Letters to Memory

Also by Karen Tei Yamashita

Letters to
Memory

KAREN TEI YAMASHITA

COFFEE HOUSE PRESS

Minneapolis

2017

Coffee House Press books are available to the trade through our primary distributor, Consortium Book Sales & Distribution, cbsd.com or (800) 283-3572. For personal orders, catalogs, or other information, write to info@coffeehousepress.org.

Coffee House Press is a nonprofit literary publishing house. Support from private foundations, corporate giving programs, government programs, and generous individuals helps make the publication of our books possible. We gratefully acknowledge their support in detail in the back of this book.

LIBRARY OF CONGRESS CATALOGING-IN-PUBLICATION DATA

Names: Yamashita, Karen Tei, 1951– author.
Title: Letters to memory / Karen Tei Yamashita.
Description: Minneapolis : Coffee House Press, 2017.
Identifiers: LCCN 2017012423 | ISBN 9781566894876 (softcover)
Subjects: LCSH: Japanese Americans—Evacuation and relocation, 1942–1945—
    Fiction. | United States—History—20th century—Fiction. | Japanese
    Americans—Fiction. | BISAC: BIOGRAPHY & AUTOBIOGRAPHY / Cultural
    Heritage. | HISTORY / United States / 20th Century. | SOCIAL SCIENCE /
    Ethnic Studies / Asian American Studies. | BIOGRAPHY & AUTOBIOGRAPHY /
    Personal Memoirs. | GSAFD: Biographical fiction. | Epistolary fiction. |
    Historical fiction.
Classification: LCC PS3575.A44 S35 2017 | DDC 813/.54—dc23
LC record available at https://lccn.loc.gov/2017012423

Images found in this book are from the Yamashita Family Archives, courtesy of the author.

PRINTED IN THE UNITED STATES OF AMERICA

24 23 22 21 20 19 18 17   1 2 3 4 5 6 7 8

*In memory
of Kishiro and Tomi
and
their nisei children*

Contents

TO BEGIN

Dear Reader:

In 1995, while packing up the contents of her Chicago apartment in preparation to move to a retirement village in California, Kay Yamashita suffered a stroke, fell into a coma, and died. When introducing herself to others elsewhere, Kay had always announced that she was from Chicago. This city seemed to be a part of her persona; she planned to have her ashes scattered across Lake Michigan. I thought she would never leave Chicago, and she didn't. Chizu, older sister and close companion, flew to be with Kay until she died. I, too, took a flight from Los Angeles, wanting to be with my two Chicago aunties one last time. Probably every cousin of my generation at some point lived with or was hosted by Chiz and Kay in Chicago. Some of us got jobs at Cook County Hospital, where Chiz was a nurse. We toured the Chicago Art Institute as guest members; enjoyed invites to the opera, ballet, or symphony; were feted in restaurants beyond our means, taken shopping to improve our wardrobe, and instructed on which wine and what dinner course; and in short, were reminded constantly that Chicago was not a hick town but a cosmopolitan center of art, culture, architecture, and politics. Now that I think about it, I realize it wasn't really Chicago as chic city that mattered so much as Kay's relationship to it, her assumption of urbanity and stylish elegance.

When I arrived at Kay's fourteenth-floor studio apartment at Sandburg Terrace, I found that its carefully spare decor of Asian art and furnishings was now a packed clutter of boxes. Where, I wondered, had all this stuff been stored in that tiny apartment? I slept on the large sofa at one end of the room, and Chiz slept on the small twin bed at the other. Between us was a maze of disorganized hoarding. Awoken in the middle of the night, I wandered around her life's accumulation—photos, books, cards, magazines, art, clothing, taxes, dishes, knickknacks, souvenirs. It was all too much, this boxing and discarding. The doorman had found her crumpled in the corridor near the door, unable to escape. In the dark, squeezing between boxed walls, I found my way to the other side of the room where Chiz slept. I stood there watching her, puzzled as to why I felt so lost. Suddenly Chiz awoke, astounded, seeing me standing in my nightgown like a dumb little kid. She sat up and grabbed me, embraced me with urgency, and I found myself enfolded in safety and sadness.

In the next days, among the stacks of Kay's stuff, we found two manila folders containing onionskin copies of typed letters. One folder was a set of letters addressed to nisei students relocated during the war from camps to colleges and universities outside of the West Coast. This was Kay's wartime work for Nisei Student Relocation. The second folder contained personal correspondence; this folder I slipped away for myself. I did not ask permission, but I also did not really read the letters until many years later, after the passing of the last of the seven Yamashita siblings: Chizu, three years after Kay in 1998, and sister Iyo in 2004.

What all of us children of the Yamashitas discovered is what every partner, child, designated relative, or friend understands about the dead: they leave stuff behind, and, depending, it could be a lot—a lifetime of stuff. When my cousins figured out that I could somehow be a useful repository of the past, they began to send me, well, everything. Boxes and envelopes arrived, piled up, the musty air of attics and garages seeping forth. When I got the university library special collections involved, my sister, Jane Tomi, exclaimed, *This is brilliant!* and unloaded more stuff. Gradually, we collected an archive of our parents' correspondence—this residue of their thinking and writing lives shared across the world and now across time.

Today, there is certainly much more in this archive than the original wartime letters. Hundreds of photographs and documents, pamphlets and paintings, homemade films and audiotapes and gramophone records, and diaries have been added. You may examine and peruse this material for yourself. For myself, I have extracted a sliver of this record to ponder some questions. I admit mine is a different or particular way of reading and seeing our story, and I ask only for your curiosity and careful intelligence. Reader—gentle, critical, or however, I count on you, as another guide through this labyrinth.

With respect,

Letters to Memory

LETTERS TO
Poverty

Dear Homer:

I am remembering when I first met you. You are sitting at a table in Kelly's bakery café with coffee and a stack of blue books, reading and scribbling comments. I have not seen a blue book in decades, but it makes sense that you would utilize this classic pedagogical format, despite penmanship's decided wane. Of course we've met before, but those meetings were encounters of a mostly bureaucratic substance, allowing me however to wave a hello and to ask the obvious question: What are you doing?

You answer that your class is on the history of sin and, you add—*by richochet*—on sacrifice and grace. I ponder the guilty rebound of sacrifice and grace and my wonder that sin has a history. But you are a historian of ancient Palestine. Of course, I think, if you say so, sin must have a history. In any case, most immediately, I am perhaps like your students, for whom sin is possibly both passé and nasty. In Brazil, they say there is no sin below the equator. But without sin, is there no sacrifice or grace? Whatever the nature of the perhaps feverish condensation of thinking in those blue books, I am moved to add my own. Similarly, seeing your stack of blue books, I am reminded of my own guilty responsibility to my own stack of my father's sermons and seminary papers. Also likely full of sin and sacrifice and grace. How should I read to understand them? You ask to what denomination did my father belong? Methodist. Ah, you consider. Forgiveness, you suggest. It is a very powerful idea.

So these conversing letters began.

Continental Divide

Greetings from Colorado ~~Utah~~ !

got up to find we were traveling thru a glorious canyon - with the Colorado River running along side of us I'm feeling a lot better today - and not so nauseated - Mom acts like a seasoned traveler and seems to enjoy everything - at the moment she is moving away - mid-morn nap.

We've been having fair weather all along - I wasn't able to enjoy very much yesterday but really there wasn't much to see - Nevada - at least what we saw of it, is desolate wasteland and Utah - what we saw of it was miles of white salt bed

Homer, today, April 30, happens to be the day on which, over seventy years ago in 1942, my father and his family lost their freedom upon entry to Tanforan Racetrack, a designated Assembly Center in San Bruno, California, for the wartime removal of Japanese. Arriving by bus, heavily encumbered with what they could carry, they were housed in a series of empty horse stalls named Barrack 14. This was just the first stop; from Tanforan they would be transported by train into the Utah desert to live in a concentration camp named Topaz. That year my father turned thirty, the fourth of seven siblings, the three elder married with children.

Five days later, my father's issei mother, Tomi, and youngest sister, Kay, were given permission to leave Tanforan. Despite their registered labels— Tomi as enemy alien and Kay as non-alien citizen—Tomi and Kay were granted passage across the continent to Washington, D.C.—Kay to testify in a federal court case regarding treason and Tomi as her companion and chaperone. A map of their cross-country trek reads like a tourist pamphlet: Grand Canyon, New Orleans, Washington D.C., New York, Boston. On May 9, Kay and Tomi were traveling on the *Scenic Limited* of the Denver & Rio Grande Western Railway between Salt Lake City and Denver. Tomi snored into her nap, but a nauseated Kay documented this passage:

> *Just went past a place where there seemed to be feverish building of barrack-like houses. The porter whispered in my ears that it's to be used for a concentration camp—beautiful country but God how terribly lonely and cold with real communion with nature and not a speck of civilization in sight.*

Reading this, I don't know whether to cry or to laugh. I think Kay has taken the train to see her future, that the Negro porter has quietly suggested, when you get to your destination, not to come back. Keep going. But Kay is only twenty-four years old, just graduated from Cal Berkeley. Her observations are not clairvoyant but innocent. *Gee,* she says, Mom and I are living the *life of O'Reilly,* complete with private Pullman and porter. It occurs to me that this might be because the other passengers object to sharing space with Japanese, not to mention Tomi's thunderous snoring. Only *a good looking real young matron* on her way to New York, mentions Kay, shares the car with them. Could be an FBI escort with cotton in her ears. In those years, who is O'Reilly and what does *real* mean?

I read and reread the letter, the jumping pulse of Kay's characteristic and enthusiastic pen flitting across the pages. I study the map. Colorado River. Iron and zinc mining. Snow. Continental Divide. Tennessee Pass, elevation = 10,240 feet. The *concentration camp* under construction that spring of 1942 must have been Camp Hale in Pando, built to house German prisoners of war and sixteen thousand soldiers, mostly of the Tenth Mountain Division, trained in skiing and winter warfare. In my first reading, I assumed the camp to be the Amache or Granada Japanese internment camp, but Amache was located on the eastern end of Colorado, not along the tracks of the *Scenic Limited* on its approach to Denver. I'm amused by my desire for irony, but the facts don't add up. Well, the porter was mistaken, though only about the location.

But there is something entirely screwball about Kay's letter, read in the context of her siblings' replies and descriptions of their shameful, stinky, muddy, hungry, bleak imprisonment. There's a shiny, foolish airhead optimism and an uncomfortable patronage of the porter, *his refined face black as night.* The Pullman porter is guide and geographer. *Holy Cats!* says Kay. *Snow!* An Oakland girl who'd never seen snow. There, on the Continental Divide, the train pauses, and the porter rushes into frozen air to scoop the white filigree into a ball, Kay marvels, *like a snow cone.*

I could choose another passage in this archive of saved stuff. Well, you choose. Kay's sister-in-law Kiyo inscribes in her diary: *Today (April 30) was one of the worst, if not the worst day I have ever experienced in my life.* Or sister Iyo writes back, *Someone we know "cracked up" one nite . . . Many a Nisei go around muttering the preamble of the Constitution, the Bill of Rights, etc.* But for me, this tableau in the Colorado Rockies sticks: civil society in anxious, tentative peace, cast on a shield against the roil of war.

We will never know the porter's name or his story, except that he had a friend named Tanaka back in L.A. But I extend a story for this gentle man that connects him to the Brotherhood of Sleeping Car Porters and to its founder and president, A. Philip Randolph.

In 1941, as the United States beat its drums for war, Randolph threatened a march on Washington. He promised to rally a hundred thousand Negroes to protest job discrimination and segregation in the armed forces. To defuse this possibility, FDR quickly signed Executive Order 8802, prohibiting discrimination in defense jobs or government. Jim Crow segregation of the military would have to wait. As the Japanese were evacuated from the West Coast, African Americans moved into their now-empty neighborhoods to take lucrative jobs in the war industry. In the few weeks that Kay traveled outside, she witnessed this influx of workers in search of jobs. The engine of war cranked into high gear to build the ships, planes, tanks, guns, bombs, parachutes, uniforms, medical supplies—all hauled off with young soldiers to theaters of battle across the Atlantic or the Pacific. Nihonmachi became the Harlem of the West.

Yet, you the historian might ask, what of significant dates? Did the war begin on December 7, 1941, on a Day of Infamy? Or perhaps on September 5, 1905, upon the signing of the Treaty of Portsmouth and Japan's defeat of Russia? Can it begin on April 30 as barbed wire fenced in one family among hundreds at Tanforan? Your scholarship teaches me that the war began centuries before. But for the short three generations of a family narrative and the story that puzzles me, there is May 9, 1942, on the Continental Divide when a ball of snow was exchanged with unspoken recognition and mistaken geography, paths crossing toward hope and sorrow.

Traitors

9

History, gently you remind me and urge me back. I have told myself, since I am prone to write fiction, that history and knowing what really happened is necessary because someone has to be accountable. Yet how close can anyone get to history even if you live it? Reading these letters, I still don't know. Stories blossom as a kaleidoscope, a space where events aggregate in infinite designs. You, Homer, hold history, its archaeology and physical evidence, with profound respect. This is the real stuff from which social systems are made. Here, you gesture, is the land and its infertility, the ruins of aqueducts and temples, the bones and seeds, here the tablets of record, an accounting of sheep and sacks of grain, progeny and slaves, tithes and taxes—basic economies that herald the complex transactions that infuse their systems into our being, initiate another future. The minutiae of every-day life congregated in patterns and traditions to account for well-being. In such a world, what does it mean to have, but more profoundly, what does it mean not to have or to lose? By what rights does one take or borrow from another? How does one come to know the difference between taking and receiving? How do greed and generosity grow and dance together? It is sinful, unlawful to steal. Failure to repay a debt may be punished. Thus the question of forgiveness is, at its basis, economic. At this moment, you also remind me, history turns to parable because to forgive debt is a radical idea, an impossibility that requires imagination.

On May 9, Kay was en route to Washington, D.C., summoned to testify on behalf of the United States on May 14, 1942, at 9:45 a.m., in the case of the *United States v. David Warren Ryder, et al.* For $152.25 plus a $6.00 processing and mailing fee, the National Archives mails me a packet of 203 legal-sized pages, the residue of criminal docket #69201, the entire extant record of a case of treason filed against Ralph Townsend, David Warren Ryder, Frederick Vincent Williams, Tsutomu Obana, K. Takahashi, and S. Takeuchi for their participation in the Jikyoku Iinkai or Japanese Committee on Trade and Information, with the alleged purpose of disseminating Japanese propaganda without registration as "foreign agents" under the Foreign Agents Registration Act of 1938. This mass of paper is a repetitive record of indictments, summons, warrants, bail amounts, jury instructions, and final judgments. There are no records of testimonies or depositions, no court banter. From this evidence, it's hard to decipher what crime had been committed except to fail to register and to make transparent a pro-Japanese position. A cursory investigation shows that both

Ryder's and Obana's early articles, published in the 1920s and 30s, are cited even today to demonstrate the unfair character of that era's anti-Japanese fears and policies in California. By 1942, however, uncritical responses to events such as the Nanking massacre, the occupation of Manchuria and Korea, and finally the bombing of Pearl Harbor would seal guilty convictions.

In 203 pages, Kay's participation is a single document: her summons to court. And nowhere in any of the dense archive of family correspondence can I find any information about why Kay was summoned and to what she testified.

What was Kay to these prominent men? Ryder was the publisher-editor of the pamphlet *Far Eastern Affairs*. Williams was a *Japan Times* newspaper correspondent, policy lecturer, and radio pundit. Of the Japanese nationals, Obana was secretary of the San Francisco Japanese Chamber of Commerce; Takahashi was manager of the steamship line Nippon Yusen Kaisha; and Takeuchi, manager of Mitsubishi Company.

Kay, the young president of the Cal Berkeley Nisei Student Women's Club with its modest membership. And Kay, a member of the Cal YM/YWCA. Years later in an interview, Kay explained that, in October 1940, she organized a campus meeting about the Japanese presence in Manchuria, inviting speakers for Chinese and Japanese viewpoints. After all, she minored in Oriental History. The Japanese Consulate provided a speaker who then became ill; the substitute speaker was one of the accused men. Was Kay asked to distribute copies of *Far Eastern Affairs* around Cal? Did Kay characterize the speech as propaganda? Knowing Kay and the sometimes Shirley Temple earnestness of her letters, it's impossible to assume any intrigue or scandal; here she stumbled unwittingly into conspiracy or, rather, suspicion. Yet in a small community, everyone's lives overlapped. Her oldest brother, Sus, worked for Mitsubishi, and S. Takeuchi was his boss. An elegant photo shows that Mr. and Mrs. Takeuchi acted as nakoodo for Sus's wedding, that is, the Takeuchis acted as formal marriage intermediaries. And Sus's wife, Kiyo, had been secretary to Obana. What, for me, is tragicomic is that Kay, a non-alien citizen, and her enemy alien mother, whose entire people had been incarcerated for alleged possible treason, were permitted free passage to testify against others for treasonable acts. The experience of testifying at the trial must have been terrifying and confusing, Kay stuttering her answers nervously, interrupted repeatedly by judicial protest, and glancing at the particular defendant, who never looked up to meet her eyes. Who did these men see on the witness stand, the only person of Japanese descent (for whom these defendants labored and suffered this humiliation) summoned to court? I doubt that her testimony sealed their fates, but even if it played a small supporting role, what cruel irony to send this sweet, young nisei woman to assert her American privilege.

Takahashi and Takeuchi escaped to Japan, soon to be surrounded by the terror of war, but Obana, educated in the United States and having spent twenty years of his life here, was imprisoned in "an alien detention camp," perhaps eventually Topaz. Years later, we read FBI files that reveal that Kay's older brother Sus had been under surveillance for his job with Mitsubishi. One report describes Sus, *the subject*, as *very intelligent . . . the dapper, smooth type*. It was Sus's responsibility to close the offices after his Japanese manager, Takeuchi, returned to Japan. A letter addressed to Special Agent T. C. Gleysteen, dated April 11, 1942, reveals that Sus's friend and coworker made a detailed report of their conversation. Visiting Sus at home, his coworker writes, that Sus *was in his garden, relaxing, he told me. He was glad to see me, and we sat in his living room along with his wife and his baby daughter. And the conversation among us went along as follows: [. . .]*

I: *"Isn't this war disgusting? And what do you think we can do in the future? Do you think we can make a go of ourselves in the United States . . . where citizenship means nothing for us?"*

He: *"Futility of war was pictured to us by the last war [. . .] What I am worried about is our second generation or 'nisei' future. I can see nothing but dark clouds. Although I feel that the United States may give us our status back, I feel that it may be best for us to go back to Japan or China and start all over again there."*

I: *"No matter what happens I am going to have faith in my government, and I am going to stay here. Where else can you find a land where people of all nationalities, races and creeds live together in apparent harmony? Of course, there are prejudices and injustices against minority, but what can anybody expect for a comparatively short time that our country was existing. Naturally, I hold a great deal of concern about our future welfare, but I think, our faith in our government will be rewarded."*

He: *"You had that conviction ever since I can remember."*
[. . .]

I: *"Will you work under the similar conditions existed at the time of our last employment? Subordinate to those from Japan, taking orders from them and at a salary way below theirs?"*

He: "I may have to. But I believe the company will make some kind of adjustment. What about you?"

I: "I certainly will not unless we are given better treatment and more authority. [. . .] You know that I offered to quit many times, and it is only the trust in your words that you will get the management to improve our situation that I plugged on."

He: "I know that, and sometimes I regret that I put you into such a misery."

I: "Please don't misunderstand me. [. . .] Although I did not enjoy working under the head accountant, I am grateful for the many friendships that I made [. . .]"

He: "I am glad that you did."

Sus's coworker closes his letter report with these words: *I felt that I have failed in my mission. I was unable to get any information out of him. But, when I reflect upon my past relationship and association with him, I noted that he had a peculiar knack, shall I say, of making others speak without letting himself be known. When I went to ask him to see whether this and that could be done, I would always come back emptying my thoughts to him without getting anything tangible from him.*

The three white Americans in the Ryder et al. case were convicted and imprisoned, it seems, for much of the war years. These men maintained their innocence; they were writing, they said, to advocate peace.

A page in the court papers reads:

Defendant Ryder's Instruction No. 6

You are instructed as a matter of law that Defendant Ryder had a constitutional right to oppose the entry of the United States in to the war with Japan and to publish writing in an effort to keep the United States out of participating in said war. Hence, even though the evidence shows that Defendant Ryder received money, still if he did nothing more than express his own sincere beliefs, you must find Defendant Ryder not guilty.

Denied, T.A.G.

The law is specific. It is not about constitutional rights or belief. It is only about registration to write propaganda, even if you believe your own propaganda. The law was created to catch the bad guys, not to quibble with what kind of bad. These instructions were denied; Ryder could not be judged innocent. In my own reading of *Far Eastern Affairs*, Ryder's punditry favored Japan's imperial incursions into China to stop the tide of what he called *Stalinist Bolshevism*. Ryder was a zealous anticommunist, and the policies he proposed in 1938 would come to pass anyway as the war came to a close. But Ryder could not be judged as peaceful.

Homer, your travels and research trace the deep history of families into tribes and tribes into nations. Some folks reach across a fence or an ocean and discover they are holding hands with the enemy. Some discover that they are on the wrong side of the fence and are the enemy themselves. Flags force everyone to flex their loyalty, but some refuse, and they are the enemy too. In this tale of the alleged traitor, all possible enemies pose a threat and must be safely imprisoned: propagandists, collaborators, apologists, aliens, non-alien citizens, renunciants, draft resisters, conscientious objectors, pacifists, expatriates, repatriates, extraordinary renditions. At the war's end, released to freedom, forgiveness is a radical idea, an impossibility that requires imagination.

I have asked myself why the family saved these letters. You might say that they were historians, that they knew the value of their stories, this proof of their thoughts and actions in unjust and difficult times. History is proffered to the future. *This is what we did. Do not forget us. Please forgive us.*

District Court of the United States for the District of Columbia

THE UNITED STATES

vs.

No. __69201__ CRIMINAL DOCKET

_____ DAVID WARREN RYDER, et al _____

5-7 - 19

The President of the United States to __Miss Kiya Yamashita, 670 - 19th Street,__

__Oakland, California.__

RECEIVED

U.S. Marshal
San Francisco, Calif.

You are hereby commanded to attend the said court on __Thursday, May 14, 1942__, at 9:45 o'clock A. M., to testify on behalf of the United States, and not depart the Court without leave of the Court or District Attorney.

Witness, The Honorable Chief Justice of said Court,

the __8th__ day of __April__, A. D., 19__42__

CHARLES E. STEWART, *Clerk.*

By _____, *Assistant Clerk.*

16—9978

Charity

One question can occupy a lifetime. What is poverty, Homer? However defined, you point out, it depends on notions of the social, moral judgment, and responsibility. What rights do people have to labor and to the fruits of the earth? If poverty is undesirable, what is our duty?

Meticulously, you research ancient records for historical, ethnographic, archaeological, literary evidence to describe what people ate, wore, cultivated, and under what sun and over what terrain, and with what traditions. You want to find the point in history when poverty becomes both a religious and political issue. Poverty may be interpreted as God's wrath and the state's injustice—but, you argue, it still affects real lives of real people. Poverty came to be understood as a lack of justice, and the idea of charity, that we have a duty to help the poor, has a beginning, though an uncertain beginning. Charity, we learn, was not always assumed. It was, along with forgiveness, a radical and shocking idea.

Kay and Tomi were expected to return to Tanforan on June 2. That day, the family hung around the grandstand, its grandeur overlooking ghostly thoroughbreds among now-aimless inmates, anticipating a kind of homecoming at the finish line. Sister and mother would not arrive for another four days.

Kay sent a letter to explain. While that is lost, it seems Kay hoped to find work to remain outside. You can surmise the letter's contents from correspondence and diary notes, showing a network of relationships with religious and educational leaders who individually and collectively protested the internment and advocated on behalf of Japanese Americans. Kay and the family's connections to these folks may have developed through my father's role as youth pastor at the Oakland West Tenth Methodist Church as well as their friendships at Cal. Friendships, references, and social occasions associated with the Y and Quakers pepper her correspondence: Rev. and Mrs. Robert Giles of the Plymouth Congregational Church, Mr. & Mrs. Harry Kingman of the YMCA, Gertie Laudauer, Frida & Irwin, Leila & Lillie Margaret, Miss Hoyt & Mrs. Hunter, Syl & Goth, Joe & Betty. And Quakers Josephine and Frank Duveneck hosted, if not mothered, Kay at their spacious Los Altos ranch home, Hidden Villa. In one letter to the family at Tanforan, she wrote, *Please give Mrs. Duveneck my sun glasses, my large blue hat, my riding habit and shoes,—she will be coming to see you folks every Wednesday morning.* I have the embarrassing sense that Kay, the last Japanese American wandering around San Francisco, became the darling of progressive Christians.

And in this interim, given a thirty-five dollar scholarship to participate in a ten-day conference at Mill College's Institute of International Relations, Kay was the lone *Oriental,* representing Japanese Americans and, with Howard Thurman, the only other person of color. She wrote, *I'm positive because I've been here, the majority of the people are waking up to the fact that this undemocratic, un-American, unjust internment of citizens without cause or too solid a reason is proving to be a real stick in their ribs, and they can't talk DEMOCRACY or a JUST PEACE without this Concentration Camp, aping the Germans, which sticks out like a sore thumb, hitting them in the face.* This angry outburst was followed by Kay's expression of her enchantment at being in the center of important discussions with the educated, dedicated, and influential. She even provided a list with short bios: Irwin Abrams, Arthur Casaday, Leila Anderson, Norman Coleman, Caleb Foote, Joe Conard, Maynard Krueger, Karl Polyani, Hans Simons, Howard Thurman. Yes, they must have all agreed, Kay had important work to do.

Back at Tanforan, the family would have none of it. They called a meeting in Barrack 20 and delegated sister Chizu to write the family opinion.

If you want to make this your life purpose and willing to sacrifice _all_ for a noble cause that is one thing—but no-one knows how long this war is to last—and it may be that during this time things may happen to us and you would be helpless to be with us. If you have the conviction—that you are willing to sacrifice family ties for the _duration_ and take whatever consequences with the spirit of one devoted entirely to a single mission—we say, more power to you, my dear.

But then, in the large body of her letter, Chiz warned that, despite the good will of influential friends, no concrete job offers had been made; that working for the Feds as clerk-typist would not necessarily ameliorate their situation in camp; that life in a city alone would be difficult; that John, Iyo, and Tom were also single and penniless and required the help of the family; that Kay could become ill without support from the family; and most emphatically, that Kay could not in five days of living at Tanforan know *the true inward feeling of hearts and minds—of people who have torn themselves from all normal living—sacrificing their life work, their homes, and their rights to live as other free people . . .* Chiz was a nurse, highly competent and professional; her skills were now employed to manage and train a hospital staff in the most rudimentary conditions. She was incensed at little sister Kay's audacious innocence. What Chiz did not write she encoded in her elegant script—Kay's naiveté.

For an entire month, Kay bucked the family opinion for idealism and almost returned to Washington, D.C. She wrote back tearfully and earnestly:

> *The family and each of you mean more to me than anything in the world— and it really isn't said tritely either—and that's why it hurts me so deeply when I see you folks . . . I find myself constantly saying I've got to do something . . . And so I've decided to go—"this above all, be true to thyself" . . .*

Meanwhile, here is a story about Tomi. When Kay and Tomi returned to San Francisco from their adventures, Kay checked into a room at the Oakland YWCA. Kay had become a pro at cross-country traveling, and if she could delay returning to Tanforan, why not? Since she was on the outside, she should meet a Professor Wagner at Mills College who provided books to be sent to the camps. And there were plans afoot for Kay's future. One thing would lead to the next. Through Wagner, who was Quaker, Kay visited the Baker Street Friends Center in San Francisco and met the embrace of Josephine Duveneck. And then there was Joe Conard, soon to be installed in Japantown on Sutter Street, working out the tedious bureaucracy of Student Relocation, that is, the project to relocate and situate Japanese American students in colleges and universities outside of the West Coast.

As she left the YWCA hotel, Kay might have advised Tomi: *Mama, stay here. I will be right back, okay?* Perhaps Kay became delayed or so involved in her meeting that she forgot about her mother. In any case, hungry, Tomi left her room and wandered out in search of food. Someone reported seeing a Japanese woman freely walking the streets. *Aren't those people all supposed to be locked up? Of course I know the difference between a Japanese and a Chinese. We Filipinos know.* When Kay returned: no Tomi. Following Tomi's trail, she found her mother sitting in the police station. What might Tomi have protested to the police? *My English is very broken. Long time I live here in Oakland. Just wait. My daughter has a paper.* Tomi was no pushover; she had had enough of traveling and chaperoning. She had seen Bourbon Street, the Lincoln Memorial, the Japanese collection at the Boston Fine Art Museum, the Statue of Liberty, and the Grand Canyon. She must have had some choice Japanese words for Kay, making it clear that she would return to Tanforan. Tanforan might be horse stalls, but there were no bars.

Well, it's a good story, but I want proof that it happened. I want to see the mug shots. On June 6, Tomi rejoined the family in Barrack 20.

Chiz had prefaced her letter to Kay: *We appreciate the many important contacts of key people you've made who are interested in what is happening and what is being actually done in these assembly centers—Tanforan in particular. We also realize the weight of their influence and position and their encouragement to you . . .* Whatever the family privately said about those *key people* under whose influence Kay moved, John might have urged Chiz to tread lightly because people of conscience were called upon in dark times to risk their lives and reputations. It was not an easy matter in a time of war hysteria and intense racial hatred to mobilize brotherhood and charity. Their Japanese American lives were tied to those who would give aid, who would come weekly to the grandstand to offer packages of food and clothing, cleaning supplies, crayons and books, pianos, butter, medical supplies, knitting wool. Tied to outsiders who would not forget.

Your story, Homer, arises from a small Catholic farming village in Northern Brittany, brought up in a Celtic language distant from Paris. A cultural cocoon of assumed practices, traditions, spiritual lives, woven into the daily and the seasonal, proprieties and conventions in which you participate without question. One day, you leave and you realize that it was theater. Everything you have known shifts. It's a terrible freedom. Everywhere you roam, you can see it. All the world is a stage. For you, the problem is to separate the fiction from the fact of living, to excavate the origins of our attachments to meaning, the material forensics of human systems, the fork in the road where we could have taken another path. This is the work of history.

But even if you trace the origins of forgiveness and charity to the self-centered and expanding exchange of goods, what about Chiz's admonishment to Kay that she might *sacrifice family ties for a noble cause*? What about the Quakers at the gate? If no one met, insiders with outsiders, at the grandstand, Kay learned to believe, forgiveness would be an impossibility. At the moment she embarked on her journey to Washington, D.C., meeting those along the railway who would give her shelter and a sympathetic ear to her story, her education began. And for a little over a month, Kay wandered outside the gates with a small crew of folks—among them gadflies, independent thinkers, honest or simply well meaning, all who probably unknowingly reached back into deep time for the significance of charity.

A month later, Kiyo's diary recorded: *July 13: Cloudy . . . Kay came back today. She is going to stay with us permanently now.*

Shortly before her return, Frank Duveneck accompanied Kay to the Whitcomb Hotel, the San Francisco headquarters for the Western Defense Command. He waited patiently for six hours as Kay was interrogated, only to discover that she and Tomi, from the very moment they embarked on their *life of O'Reilly* to their reentry into Tanforan, had been *tailed.* The southern colonel who encouraged and created the travel plans that routed them to see his home state of Texas, Bourbon Street, Jim Crow, and southern hospitality, had perhaps another purpose. The letters show Kay to have been oblivious to this purpose, though back at Tanforan, she intimated, the inmates gossiped that she must have been out there for a reason, possibly as a stooge for the Feds.

Many years ago, you gathered boxwood from the garden, walked with your family to church for Palm Sunday blessings. On the path, you placed sprigs of boxwood in the mossy embankments and at home in the shed with the cows and horses. This is the memory of your childhood village that later becomes transparent as theater. Still it is a *magic world.* And Kay, having returned to Tanforan after three weeks, writes to the outsiders, describing *the real miniature gardens with wishing wells, ponds (made by lining them with tar paper or the clay that is found here) with goldfish shaped from carrots, rock gardens, flower beds, vegetable gardens and window boxes . . . temporary as these places are, it is amazing how homey . . .* I realize that for my family the automatic and habitual of their prewar childhoods had been entirely overturned. A terrible way to be freed to new knowledge and to change. But this is fiction.

<u>REBURIAL SERVICE OF NOBU KAJIWARA</u>
at GOLDEN GATE NATIONAL CEMETARY - SAN BRUNO, CALIFORNIA
March 11th, 1949 - 2:00 P.M.

HAPLAIN PRESIDING:- Opening Words and Scripture

MILY MINISTER: Biography and Remarks   Rev. John Yamashita

Private 1st Class Nobuo Kajiwara of Company B - 100th Battalion, later
t Battalion of the 442nd Infantry, joined the 100th Battalion in Italy in
rch 1944 — Saw action at Anzio, in the Battle of Rome, at Leghorn and Livorno,
id the supreme sacrifice near the Arno River on the Pisa Offensive in Italy on
ly 11th, 194

Born in Oakland, California in September 5th, 1914, he has come back now —
s remains to rest in these hills underneath the fair sky in these environs
ere he enjoyed his youth, spent the leisure days of recreation, which he
ved so well, and to which he hoped to return.

He represents the many hundreds of others — who trained arduously in
eat at Camp Shelby and elsewhere and ventured into the grime and blood of
tion — saw "the hell and high water" of war — once which their eyes see
ey never speak of — who gave of his life without reservation — going from
rbed wire camp on a mission to declare the freedom and dignity of man.
the words of the Citation signed by the President Franklin Delano Roosevelt
he "dared to die that freedom might live and grow and increase its blessings.
eedom lives and through it He lives in a way that humbles the undertakings
most men."

We thank God for his life as a babe and a child, and the tears and laugh-
r that he gave to his parents in their years of loving nurture — We thank
d for his life as a brother and friend, the companionship he shared with his
sters and friends in his youth — We thank God for his earnest idealism which
d him to loyal and faithful participation in a cause he believed in. Ours
the priceless and noble heritage — with tender regard and loving care we
mit his remains to the good earth here.

We pray this day for the family. Give them encouragement and strength
the hour that they mourn the loss of their only son. May they know that:
o man is an Island entire of itself: every man is a piece of a continent,
art of the main; if a clod be washed away by the sea, Europe is the less...
" man's death diminishes me, because I am involved in mankind". The rest
Nobu is his friends, his country and its ideals he loved. As part of him
ll you feel free to call upon us his friends who have here gathered to pay
ir tribute — call upon us anytime, anywhere in your hour of need and we
l be honored to share his friendship with you, his family.

RAYER -   -Rev. Shigeo Shimada

PLAIN'S COMMITTAL - VOLLEY AND BUGLE CALL

SENTATION OF THE FLAG - ARMY PALLBEARERS ESCORT TO FINAL RESTING PLACE

23

Homer, you spoke about a one-substance world, a world in which mortals and deathless gods coexist, a rich Hellenic past, font of Western rationality. However, you argue, it is when that one-substance world is abolished, when the panoply of gods are sent packing for a one-god/two-substance split between the secular and spiritual, that a truly rational world is set in place. God may exist or not exist as an idea, as an abstraction, and there is no returning, I think, except by fiction, by imagination.

The *Iliad* is a book of war. It's a tale with mythic consequences embedded in the literature I love, but I'm embarrassed to have gotten this far without actually reading it. By the way, it's a prize-winning translation. I lug the heavy volume onto a transcontinental flight, SFO to DCA, and crack the spine. I sip a Bloody Mary and order a seven dollar snack box of nuts, string cheese, and stick salami, and settle in for the duration. All right, so this is my *life of O'Reilly*. The guy next to me is reading a Tom Clancy novel on his Nookie. Surely Clancy has read the *Iliad*. It predates the Chinese *Water Margin* by centuries, and if you want splashing blood and erupting guts, move over Kurosawa, spaghetti Westerns, and Tarantino. I'll need another Bloody Mary, please. The Nookie's been turned off in favor of the sky-falling 007, but I cannot be pried away. I admit, perhaps like other unsuspecting readers, I turn the pages expecting to encounter the Trojan horse and Achilles's heel. Fate, the inevitability of mortal death can only be tampered with. In a one-substance world, the important rules are the same for mortals and immortals. Inevitably, Troy will fall, despite the interventions of the gods—the manipulations of Queen Hera and Achilles's mother Thetis, the rage of Athena sprung from the head of King Zeus, Aphrodite's wicked love. The horse and the heel and even Helen are unimportant to this story about the terrible pride of two men, Achilles and Hector, fated to wage war and die in gruesome battle. In one transcontinental flight, the tragic fate of Troy is held aloft in the mind of the reader. Knowing Fate, do we secretly cheer for the winners, those great Achaeans? The legendary Troy with its great walls fortressing the House of Priam was located at the mouth of the Dardanelles connecting the Aegean Sea to the Sea of Marmara in what is now Turkey. I look up at the screen; somewhere in a stone chapel in a bleak Scottish countryside, 007 is cradling the dying M. Neither 007 nor M really believe in God, but they are still, you will say, the reckless consequences of the fall of Troy.

If it can be dated, maybe thirty centuries after the Trojan War, you arrived in San Francisco from Northern Brittany via Jerusalem and walked from the Financial District through the Tenderloin to the Federal Building. Your epiphany, gazing upward into the great glass and steel structures of money and power and walking through littered streets among the impoverished, was that even you—a child of peasant farmers, tenants—sensed, as a white man, ownership. This feeling you defined as imperial. It was knowledge that perhaps only you as an outsider could know so directly. You saw all your experiences, embodied in a convergence of Catholicism, Judaism, and Islam, transformed. From that moment, perhaps you understood your responsibility to dismantle that worldview, to become, I believe, a gadfly at the gate of war.

Of the Yamashita family, youngest son Tom, nephew Ted, and brother-in-law Min were drafted into the Army, but fortunately the war was ending, and their duties and placements were not in combat. Kimi's son Ted joined military intelligence and served during the occupation years in Tokyo until 1952. Drafted around 1943, Tom was sent to Ohio State University to the army's advanced engineering program, whose personnel fed the Army Corps of Engineers and the Manhattan Project. Apparently, very abruptly, Tom was released from the program, separated from his white colleagues, and sent to Fort Polk in Louisiana, spending the rest of the war, he said, *pumping gas.*

Sus's diary entry in New York: *Tuesday, August 7: Clear . . . News of the atomic bombing of Japan on Monday, August 6 came today.* And three days later: *Friday, August 10: Clear-cool . . . One of the most memorable days in my life. Got the news of Japan's proposing to surrender unconditionally late this afternoon . . . How glad our parents must be now that they are sure of seeing their sons coming home without even a single injury during their service!*

Throughout my growing years, I remember a sepia portrait of the handsome face of a young man with a pipe. This photograph always hung in John's study. I think I was a troubled sleeper, and I would show up in the middle of night or early morning and find my dad pounding away at the typewriter or staring into his thoughts or at this photo, usually writing his Sunday sermon at the last moment. I suspect the pipe was a photographic affectation of the time; I now know the portrait was of Nobuo Kajiwara, John's childhood buddy and classmate at Cal.

Nobu had two sisters, Michi and Sachi. He was the only son. Like most of the Oakland folks, the Kajiwaras were shipped out to Topaz. John recalled that Nobu *quarreled vehemently* with his parents about his decision to enlist. In March 1943, Nobu wrote to his sisters who had then moved to Lincoln, Nebraska:

> *I know this will shock you. I have volunteered to join the armed forces and will be part of the combat unit . . . A unit coming up spontaneously and not of duress (as in draft) will get far better publicity. Publicity organized and of the right kind, will be in favor of all Japanese sincerely wishing to remain in the U.S. And it is only by such positive action that the country will open up decent jobs for a decent living. Sounds idealist—I'd be the first to say that such a reformation of American public opinion will not come about overnight. It'll take years but just consider the position of you and me and the rest of the nisei if no action were taken. I don't like the set up any more than you do and there is the further discomforting thought that I may never come back. But to be honest with myself and to keep what self respect I do have . . .*

The Kajiwaras and the Yamashitas were both Christian families. They were not taught to hate the enemy, but pacifism would not be an option. Nobu enlisted in the Japanese American segregated unit, the 100th Battalion. On his way to Italy, he stopped in Chicago to see his old friend John one last time. John wrote, *I can remember when I was told that Nobu was felled in that fight to cross the Rapido River just north of Rome.* And his words stop there.

In the *Iliad*'s poetic history, when the offended and brooding Achilles refuses to fight, his dearest friend, Patroclus, wearing Achilles's armor, rallies the Achaeans and dies by the sword of Hector. Enraged, Achilles returns to battle and kills Hector. Hector's death, like every other death in this book, is graphically described: *one spot lay exposed, where the collarbones lift the neckbones off the shoulders, the open throat . . . Achilles drove his spear and the point went stabbing clean through the tender neck . . .* But it is the pyre that Achilles creates to burn Patroclus's corpse that amazes me. Sacrificed are *droves of fat sheep and shambling crook-horned cattle* whose fat is flayed to wrap the corpse. Then, *two-handled jars of honey and oil,* the bodies of *four massive stallions,* two dogs—throats slit, and a *dozen brave sons of the proud Trojans* hacked to pieces—all this atop timber stacked *a hundred feet in length and breadth,* and Achilles on a chariot, dragging Hector's body to and fro. Somewhere in this pile of death is the body of Patroclus.

I discover an interview with Ken Kaname Takemoto, who trained with Nobu at Camp Shelby in Hattiesburg, Mississippi, and landed together at Anzio:

> [Nobu] was attacking a German position. The story I heard was that he was about to lob a grenade. He had pulled the pin—you know, a grenade has a safety pin attached to it, and once you pull the pin you have to hold the handle down so it won't go off. If you release it, you have three seconds to get rid of it. You count "one, two, three," and throw it. So he had pulled the pin, but before he could get rid of it, he was shot. His hand released the grip, and the grenade exploded. His own grenade. Blasted him . . . he didn't die right away—he was in such pain that he ran around screaming until he collapsed and died. So it was a horrible death.

There was another photograph that framed John in a ministerial gown behind a casket draped with an American flag. In the photo also, I recognize Nobu's sisters, Michi and Sachi, and their issei parents, a tableau in somber black. Homecoming, glory, honor, fate. Nobu's death was all of this and none of this.

Priam, king of Troy, sneaks through the battlefront with a wagonload of treasure, a king's ransom, to kneel before Achilles and plead for Hector's body. *I put to my lips the hands of the man who killed my son.* Priam has lost fifty sons to this war and now the great Hector. Achilles is moved to grieve for his own father's glory and misery, manipulated by the whims of the gods. Priam boasted fifty sons, all dead. Achilles's father sired one son, soon to die. Achilles weeps with Priam and returns the son to the father. The poet is careful; as you will remind me, it is not a moment of charity or reconciliation, but of pity and self-pity and exchange, but it is the saddest moment and the end of the book.

Poverty, you explain, can be chosen. That is its power. It occurs to me now—Kay, John, Nobu—each chose poverty.

Homer, forgive me as I have taken liberties, and I still do not understand.

For
Dear Albert —

With love,
Your grandson,
Kiyoshi

Dear Homer:

You ask, even though you had from the very beginning suggested it, even though the body of your scholarship (as I interpret it) is given to this idea: why forgiveness? I puzzle over this, but sense that it is a question from which you cannot be released. I also appreciate that your query is Socratic and teacherly, an insistence to pursue my thinking, saying that, despite your guidance, *I do not understand* is a kind of understanding. Forgiveness, you offer, requires the confrontation of two parties, a meeting face-to-face between people who have the capacity to hurt each other, and thus, perhaps, to discover grace. This is to carry the idea into practice. You translate the request, *please forgive us,* to say: *Please receive us in our fullness.* But such encounters are impossible because all the players are dead—jailers and inmates, Chizu and Kay. And what about evil, you ask. This is a much larger question.

As for history, you note the historian's problem that writing about an event is not the same as living it. History is an inquiry, and there is an attempt here to, as you say, *clear the ground with these letters,* meaning perhaps to properly bury the dead. Yet even so, you say, *we are rendered speechless, dumb, when it comes to the hearts.* There are, you agree, things beyond history, which history may point to yet also obscure. Beyond or behind history are glimpses of what matters.

You pause after the first section to note that what you recognize in this writing is *a letter about letters,* what you call an *invocation.*

You requested a clarification about Chizu's letter in which her words suggest Japanese Americans had a choice about their imprisonment; she describes *people who have torn themselves from all living—sacrificing their life work, their homes, and their rights to live as other free people.* Perhaps the words *torn* and *sacrifice* indicate free action, but no such freedom existed, even though this incarceration was called *a wartime necessity.* At the same time, it occurs to me now that Chizu's way of describing this event was in itself a refusal to be a herded prisoner, a refusal to lose dignity.

I am gratefully yours,

LETTERS TO
Modernity

Dear Ishi:

Nobody wants my brain. Even if my driver's license were to indicate my willingness to have my body parts distributed, decidedly, nobody wants my brain. There are days, when it hurts, that even I do not want my brain. It may be, however, that the FBI might want my computer. Special Collections seems to want my books and all their related detritus. And connected to that, we'll foist this family archive of letters and photographs and wartime materials on them. I asked Homer why he thought my family saved this stuff, and he responded with the historian's view that they knew what was happening to them was significant and wrong, that justice might not happen in their lifetimes. What they saved shows that this is true, but we children thought that they were nostalgic packrats. Now we are old and nostalgic ourselves and comb through this business like we invented it. We pass PDFs and HTMLs over e-mail, google this and that—amateur historians, trying to compensate for the fact that as kids we were too distracted by the idea of this past to be actually immersed in it. Shame on us. Now they are all dead, and we didn't save their brains either.

But let's be fair. To live like Walter Benjamin's angel, swept into the future while staring into the past, is pretty horrific. I salute you and Homer for being willing to do so. But what to net in this storm of wreckage and debris? There is what has been salvaged, and there is what attracts our attention. You remind me that the museum gets organized and reorganized. Each of us covets a glass case of curiosities arranged particularly. When we are dead, what meaning will it have? When I'm dead, I suspect everything in my glass case can be burned and replaced by a USB flash drive. Who cares about my brain?

But Homer's work demonstrates the tedious precision of tracing the forensics of history, to uncover a question stone by stone. To have access to those stones at all; his eyes glow with wonder. You interpret Ishi to be the Yahi word for *man*, but I also translate from the Japanese meaning *stone*. Stone by stone. Forgive me; it is taboo to speak of the dead. But they are my dead, and I fear the reasons for which they saved these letters and how here I must necessarily fail. And yet, I ask for your indulgence, to attempt to overturn at least one stone.

2151 Vine Street,
Berkeley, California
January 5, 1942

ar Kay,

is letter is coming to you as one who is actively interested in the program
the F.O.R. working with problems created by the evacuation. I hope that yo
n give it serious consideration and will be able to help me on some of the
ints below.

der separate cover, we are mailing you a copy of the December issue of
LLOWSHIP magazine, with an article, "Democracy in Detention," on life in a
location Center. Probably you have already seen this article, but there may
others in the Center whom you would like to pass this on to. I also enclos
th this a reprint of a remarkable little article by Ernest Meyers which I'm
re will interest you if you don't already know of it. If you wish additiona
pies of either of these, let me know. FELLOWSHIP, published monthly, is sen
all members of the F.O.R. and contains considerable information about the
acuation.

is Berkeley office of the F.O.R. is also going to publish a small Newsletter
r circulation among pacifists in the Camps, and you will receive a first cop
this before long. The F.O.R. group at the Coleville(California) C.P.S. Cam
going to do the mechanical work of mimeographing and mailing this Newslette
will edit future issues.

both this Newsletter and a new pamphlet on American Concentration Camps on
ch I am working, I should like to have your reactions and help on several
nts:

(1) Can you send me any further details you may have on actual life withi
relocation centers; what part the pacifist has to play in the centers;
acasian-Japanese relationships.

(2) The social and psychological effects of life in a Camp. Moving or hu
us anecdotes which could be used in print will be especially helpful.

(3) What solutions you see ahead. What would be an ideal solution? What
ution seems politically practicable?

(4) Any new information you may have gained as to the causes of the origi
evacuation (economic, propaganda, political, etc.) will be valuable.

(5) I am extremely anxious to get hold of some good pictures showing life
the Japanese in America, either before, during, or after evacuation. Can yo
p with this, for I wish to have my new pamphlet well illustrated.

ope you had a happy holiday season and that the new year may bring us a clo
roach to peace on earth and goodwill towards men.

Cordially yours,

Caleb

Caleb Foote,
Northern California Field Secretary.

loads for Ne
has greetings.
ne to hear from you in detail on Ne point

37

Independence Day, 1942. Franklin Delano Roosevelt declared that the nation would celebrate *not in the fireworks of make-believe but in the death-dealing reality of tanks and planes and guns and ships. We celebrate it also by running without interruption the assembly lines, which turn out these weapons to be shipped to all the embattled points of the globe. Not to waste one hour, not to stop one shot, not to hold back one blow—that is the way to mark our great national holiday in this year of 1942.* As he spoke, submarine USS *Triton* ejected two torpedoes from its payload, sinking the Japanese destroyer *Nenohi* in the Aleutian Islands off Alaska.

While 188 sailors churned in icy death, presumably it was a warm summer day 3,000 miles south across the Pacific, a soft breeze lifting with white gulls across a blue bay, pleasant sunlight dappling the Mills College campus, gracious lawns and tree-lined paths sweeping toward stately buildings. Kay, still at large in Oakland, wrote to the family in Tanforan about a crowd that gathered that day on the lawn outside of Lisser Hall for an open discussion on race relations, convened by Leila Anderson, general secretary of the Cal Berkeley YWCA. The day was strategic, the discussions urgent—although as Kay admitted, she was the singular oriental face in a sea of educated white folks, one last Japanese, her temporary independence protected by a dedicated core of good guys in opposition to the recent evacuation of her people.

The key organizer of this *July 4th F.O.R. Day* was a young man named Caleb Foote. Foote was a recent graduate of Harvard, former editor of the *Harvard Crimson,* and a pacifist, chosen by A. J. Muste to open a branch of the Fellowship of Reconciliation in Northern California. Until his conviction for violation of military service, Foote would work relentlessly—researching, traveling, organizing, and writing on behalf of conscientious objectors and incarcerated Japanese Americans. Exchanging correspondence with Kay in camp, one tattered form letter has survived with Foote's handwritten note at the bottom: *Thanks loads for the Christmas greetings. I'd like to hear from you in detail on the points above. You have been one of my best informants. Caleb.*

Informants. Perhaps the cultural anthropologist in you raises your eyebrows, but then, you'll sigh, this was 1943. I admit, unlike encountering *gee, golly, swell, oh boy oh boy,* or *O'Reilly,* I fidgeted over *informant.* But under these circumstances, who was going to write about or for us, if not those others?

At the very same time that Kay was sipping Cokes with anxious academics and vociferous pacifists at Mills, sociologist and demographer

Dorothy Swaine Thomas was organizing her cohort for a study of Japanese-American Evacuation and Resettlement under the auspices of the Yamashita family alma mater, Cal Berkeley, and the University of Pennsylvania. With the generosity of the Rockefeller, Columbia, and Giannini Foundations, and the cooperation of the War Relocation Authority (WRA), War Department, Western Defense Command, and Fourth Army, this study, known by its acronym JERS, produced two very informative volumes: *The Spoilage* and *The Salvage*, published by UC Press in 1946 and 1952. *The Spoilage* was co-authored with Richard Nishimoto, and *The Salvage* with the assistance of Charles Kikuchi and James Sakoda. The authors make clear the difficulties of gathering information within any prison:

> *Constant efforts had to be made to guard against betrayal of informants . . . To their fellow evacuees, "research" was synonymous with "inquisition" and the distinction between "informant" and "informer" was not appreciated. Consequently every one of our evacuee staff members was stigmatized, or in danger of being stigmatized . . .*

Despite the provocative conditions and limitations of this study, its three-year scope from 1942 to 1945 reveals a sense of immediate pain, not remembered but lived in deep frustration and contained anger. In 1945, the war was over and the study ended, and those lost years were irretrievable. Years later, we retrieve the irretrievable.

Of course you recognize the slippery path between opportunity and advocacy. If a bad thing was going to happen anyway, why depend on only diaries or letters or mere memory to keep the truth? Why not gather and organize documentation as events transpired? Social science could analyze the data, unravel the consequences, dictate appropriate future policies. So many years later, I find these justifications preposterous; the most fascist regimes have been known to keep the most meticulous accounting of their crimes. And how creepy is it to request from the National Archives the War Relocation Authority files of the Yamashita siblings and then to receive several hundred pages of incarceration documents systematically saved? A precise record and evidence of injustice served. As for the JERS archive, it is stored in the UC Bancroft Library and consists of 379 reels of microfilm, 336 boxes, 84 cartons, 36 oversized volumes, 6 oversized folders—all for a total of 250.5 linear feet of stuff. Chronologically, the miles of barbed-wire fences that corralled my family preceded the 250.5 linear feet of paper, but something in my gut tells me that the logic of this is skewed, that the science of the social had long before measured and interred the cornerstones and the supporting stakes. The very possibility of corralling a people into some kind of single tribe was born in the idea of having discovered them in the first place.

Ishi, that intuition in my gut is that which you long ago recognized as a critical *de-centering*, the gaze of another unmasked. This is the dance my folks and those who came to their aid danced together in a dark time of war and justified injustice.

They: *These people are loyal. Race has nothing to do with loyalty.*

Us: *Yes, look how loyal we are! Please notice what kind of loyal.*

They: *Only such a group of people can be this loyal in this way. They are culturally loyal.*

Us: *Yes, yes, loyalty flows in our very blood and is our birthright.*

They: *But more importantly, their loyalty has been cultivated on American soil; it's a fully assimilated loyalty.*

Us: *Our loyalty is fully assimilated.*

This is perhaps a dance that could not have been otherwise, but it is a dance that forever defines my folks, narrates who we become.

The prefaces of *The Spoilage* and *The Salvage* are instructive in laying out the intent of the study. Thomas and Nishimoto explain that *spoilage* refers to those Japanese Americans who were repatriated to Japan, stigmatized as disloyal to the United States, and segregated at the Tule Lake Center. *Salvage* refers to those Japanese Americans "whose status in America was, at least temporarily, improved through dispersal and resettlement in the East and Middle West... many participating directly in the war effort." There was a third classification, *residue,* to include the *net effects* of *spoilage* and *salvage;* that is, those classified as *spoilage* who anyway were reabsorbed into a *more tolerant America;* those as *salvage* were individuals who failed to assimilate into the American workforce through resettlement, plus those who remained in the camps until the war's end in 1945, when they were forced out finally to homelessness. If the designation *informant* bites, think about the *garbage* narrative here invoked. Waste, debris, trash, wreckage, refuse. I note here that *The Residue* is a third volume yet to be written.

The Yamashitas were for the most part the *salvage.* By the end of 1943, the seven siblings had left or were in the process of leaving Topaz. Chizu and her husband Ed and little son Kiku, who the family called Kix, moved to harvest sugar beets on a farm in Idaho. Kay found a job in Philadelphia to work for the Quakers and Nisei Student Relocation. Iyo married Min Tamaki and headed for Chicago, then Philadelphia. Tom got into the University of Nebraska in Lincoln and John into the seminary in Evanston, near Chicago. Kimi's husband Bob left to teach Japanese language to American soldiers at the University of Michigan in Ann Arbor, with Kimi and daughter Martha following later; son Ted left for college in Saint Louis. Susumu and Kiyo had the most difficult time leaving camp, and the records show that Sus was blacklisted as a kibei and former employee of Mitsubishi. By the end of the war, Sus and Kiyo had three children, two of them born in Topaz. Sus left pregnant Kiyo and two daughters behind in Topaz and went to find work while enrolling in the New York Technical Institute. Mother Tomi took up painting and became a student of the artist Chiura Obata. Despite the circumstances, for the first time in Tomi's life, she found herself released from constant labor. I realize that because of this gradual dispersal—this process of *salvage*—our archive of letters exists, the family network constantly tugging and crossing the desert camp Topaz, that jewel of a garbage dump. With this history in mind, the meaning of *salvage anthropology* for me takes a strange turn: not to salvage physical, narrative, linguistic, or practiced artifacts, but to salvage what is understood to be American.

On June 1, 1942, a month before the Independence Day discussions at Mills College, Caleb Foote wrote to John Nevin Sayre at the Fellowship of Reconciliation in New York:

> *I was very much interested and stimulated by what you wrote me about Bayard Rustin, and I feel some similar tactics must be adopted by us at this time when our democracy is going down the spout and a "ghetto psychology" created among both the Japanese minority <u>and</u> the Caucasian majority. What should these tactics be? One part is speaking out, even more openly than we have. Another, it seems to me, is direct non-violent opposition to carrying this program out. My imagination is very poor on the latter point, but I can think of a few examples, such as camping outside one of the evacuation camps, sharing their living conditions and privations, and perhaps picketing the gates; or even lying down across the entrances so that army and other evacuation officials would be made to realize what <u>they</u> are doing ... If some young people could be brought out from the East and Middle West, so that we could have, say, a total aggregation of 25, given some careful training by someone like A.J. ...*

My own feeling is that many more of the Japanese should be doing what
Gordie Hirabayashi is doing in Seattle—going to jail rather than obeying
the evacuation orders. But obviously we cannot call upon them to do this
unless we also are prepared both to offer them a way out and an example.
I also have a feeling we might do better to go to jail for something like this
than for violating Selective Service Act.

Caleb Foote's proposal for *direct non-violent opposition* did not happen,
though its possibilities were alive and planted for the future. And yet I
wonder what might have happened had twenty-five young people laid
their bodies across the gates of Tanforan or Topaz. I imagine that this
event would have been a great failure, but I want to embrace the young
man who urgently and passionately proposed such action. Foote and Rustin
believed that their pacifism was made of the boldest stuff of human integrity and courage, or it was nothing.

But to return to Foote's request from Kay for information. Kay and
others contributed in large and small ways to the results of his research to
create a pamphlet entitled *Outcasts!* Foote believed that decisions made
on the basis of racism could not ultimately hold up in a court of law based
on rights under the Constitution. The legal apparatus would turn to evidence, and the evidence demonstrated what Japanese Americans seemed
primed to represent: the most loyal and democratic Americans on Earth.
Other pamphlets about the Japanese evacuation were written and distributed, but no other so clearly connected Japanese American evacuation to the racism of Jim Crow, anti-Semitism, and the larger context of
social justice and incarceration, while also anticipating future struggles
for legal redress.

Our liberties and the sincerity of our repudiation of the monstrous
doctrine of a master race depends upon our success in removing from our
legal system the possibility that under any circumstances any Executive
can have the awful power asserted by the President in the order of
February 19, 1942, a power intended to be used against the members of
one particular race, but nonetheless applicable in stormy years to any
unpopular minority. That way lies death to our democracy.

Foote prefaces *Outcasts!* with the header "The Tyranny of a Word," the
word being *Japs,* an enemy label that negated and disparaged *our citizens,*

our Americans of Japanese descent. But what about the designations *out-cast* or *dispossessed, refugee* or *salvage*? These words, utilized by advocates and anthropologists to provoke action and empathy, also defined the shame of the Japanese American self, crafted in a dance of loyalty and disloyalty and finally performed in order to survive.

Outcasts!

The Story of America's Treatment
of Her Japanese-American Minority

BY CALEB FOOTE

15c

uru Mother,

Chiodo ten days mm tachi mashita ne -- ano Saturday naki nak
a to C hizu to wakare ta hi. Ano hitoban wa nerare nai kurai
ami mashita. Soshite mata mainichi nete mo okitemo, nanika
itemo, mete mo anatatachi no koto ga doshite mo meno mai ni
u yo u ni arimasu. Kono nagai aida tegami mo kakazu ni oru
o wa kore naun desu.

Mama ga yoku shiteru yo oni - watakushi wa chi isai toki kara
ily unit and home wa ichi ban daiji mata ichiban tou toi mono
omotsute imashita, mata ima demo nani hoka no hito kara uwarete
shi in kara so omoi masu. Ima watakushi ga shiteru koto wa
u koto wo wasure te shiteru yo u ni omoi ni naru kamo shi re
desuga --Please Mother so u dewa nai. Because I care nani ka
nai de wa orare

The Order of Benedict

Last Saturday - Kay no bakayaro to omoi ni natsu ta ka mo shi
nai - and - so de a su -- moshi koshi understanding wo
su te mi un na mo u u bo w o to na n na ya ra tsu ta to
ni natsu te omo masu watakushi to shi un mono tachi ga
un nani naru koto watakushi to shite wa ho un to u hi ta ma
nai koto desu -- mata wakushi no family da ke de wa nai -- o u
no hito tachi ga oun nashi ni ko un nani ya ra re te shi ma tsu
u koto wo ka un gai ru to -- do u shite mo iro iro ma yo ri
u -- ji bun ka ? mata ji bun wo wamu reru koto.

Last Saturday no Experience wa ki zu yori mada mada fukai
n sho wo watakushi ni o i ta.-- do-o shi te mo wasu re ru
o wa de ki nai -- wa ta kushi de, de ki ru koto ga atsu ta
doshi te mo shi koshi de mo ko no suffering, unhappiness,
stration wo remove suru koto ga motsu te mo kisku hitsu yo,
chi C amp ni oka r e ta tsu te ko to ga nayami datsu da ga
iru to ko ga so un na ni iya na to ko ro de aru to omo u to
un da WRA Camps ni itsu ta ra mata o na ju yo u na to ko de
yo u ni su ru ko to ga motsu to mo hi tsu yo u ni omo i masu.
ther da ke wa wa ta ku shi do un na ni omo te de de ki ru ga
-i teru desho. Mother da ke wa ta ku shi wo ho un to ni
nji te ku re ta ra b a - ho ka no uchi no mo no ga na ni wo
-tsu te mo de ki ru. Please Mother believe in me and God
l do the rest.

Toshi mo wa kai mata experience mo tara nai -- ho un to ni
ra nai watakushi no ko to wo Mother wa shi un pai su ru ko to
omo i masu ga -- I will do my best and what is in my heart and
en I shall be willing to return to you. Mother no kara da, mata
shi ya ra iroiro ka un gai ru to i ka nai ho ga i-i to omo i
su ke re do -- ke re do ko xmx yu koto wo ka un ga e ru to
know I must be assured that everything will be alright, and I
ow you will only be happy when everyone else is happy.

Dewa wa zu ka no ai da i tsu te ku ru. My love, my kisses,
prayers, my thoughts will always be with you.

Ishi, I have wondered about your idea that ethnography could be a *surrealist* project enacted on a *science of cultural jeopardy*. I don't imagine that my enactment here of juxtapositions, not really surreal, is necessarily what you had in mind, but it is true that this *shuffling of realities* has begun to unmake my old world. It has anyway been my creative method to contort or at least humor the mind toward revelation. I do not entirely understand your meaning—*cultural jeopardy,* a kind of anthropological game of risk taking—though I sense that I am about to lose something. If that something is my culture, it seems to always have been a dynamic thing constantly in its death throes, nearing extinction.

Perhaps I should consider hierarchical structures. In the Yamashita clan of seven, the sibling lineup was significant. The first two children, Susumu and Kimi, were sent to be educated in Japan; they were entirely bilingual kibei, returning to the United States in the decade before the war. We called them Neech and Neich, for niichan and neichan, literally older brother and older sister, the "-chan" suffix being familiar, endearing, linked to childhood. As a kid, I called them Uncle Neech and Auntie Neich; I never knew their real names until much later. The next two children were Chizu and John. Then Iyo, Kay, and Tom. Of course this is my interpretation, but Neech and Neich, having lived away from the family in Japan, seemed to be titular or honorary first son and first daughter. The practical job of elder sibling authority was assumed by Chizu and John, the first fully American daughter and son. And when the war broke out, perhaps it became understood that the kibei relationship to Japan must become quiet or invisible. But the letters themselves reveal varying degrees of formal or counselor authority and emotional dependence. Kay and Tom would always be the young ones. Iyo in her middle position, I think, was happily the most free. And this brood gathered around the widowed matriarch Tomi. The letters over many years were the necessary fabric that wove the Yamashita family together. They reveal an intense assumption of blood connection and loyalty but also the necessity of making it in the world independently.

Kay's letter to Tomi, written in Japanese romaji, suggests the crisis that may have occurred when Kay attempted to leave the family at Tanforan. In one last visit to Barrack 20, Kay may have become hysterical, and more than frank words were exchanged.

Last Saturday—what might have made Kay look foolish—no, I was—
I now wish I had understood better what I heard everyone say. Knowing

*that the people I love think of me that way is so disheartening to me . . . I
can't stop thinking about last Saturday's Experience; it left a deep impres-
sion in me. It's impossible to forget. If there's anything I could do about this,
it's doing whatever is necessary to remove this suffering, unhappiness,
and frustration . . . Only you Mother know how I feel, what I am capable
of thinking. If you trust me, I don't care what others think of me. Please
Mother believe in me and God will do the rest.*

When her brothers and sisters derided her idealism, Kay pleaded to
higher authorities: Tomi and God. My grandmother's reputation was that
she was a tough and demanding old lady, but Kay must have found refuge
there. As a grandkid, I couldn't really tell; I knew she was formidable, the
obligatory family center, and that for me she represented Japan: its language, pretensions, aesthetics, social and cultural values. Tomi was for me
a proud Edokko, my samurai grandma, the chrysanthemum and the sword.

What nisei family in the 1950s did not own a copy of Ruth Benedict's
The Chrysanthemum and the Sword? Well, perhaps that's overstated, but
I would argue that book and Harry Kitano's *Japanese Americans: The
Evolution of a Subculture,* published in 1969, were the sociological foundations for what we popularly define to be us, Japanese Americans. Benedict
gives us our variations of obligation, *on* and *giri,* our shame rather than
guilt, plus our complex idea of revenge—*Chushingura* or the *47 Ronin,*
and Kitano gives us *gaman* (perseverance), *shikataganai* (don't cry over
spilled milk), and *enryo* (ceremonious hesitation). I especially appreci-
ated that *enryo* is a *syndrome.* But it's been around a half century since
these books were published. Does anybody care about this anymore?
In fact, quite recently, the Los Angeles Japanese daily *The Rafu-Shimpo*
published an article with the obligatory lineup of *gaman* to *hazukashii:
Caregivers: Japanese Americans at Risk.* Make sure your non-JA in-laws
read this so they understand the intricacies of caring for us as we all ease
into Alzheimer's.

I check out a library copy of Benedict's book, microdust rising off the
yellowing and acid-eaten pages. I cough, comforted by the thought that
I'm similarly allergic to my family's archive of letters. It's all dust from
the same period. These days I tuck Benedict into my bag and snatch paragraphs while sitting with my mother Asako at the hospital. She is ninety-
six years old and, by marriage, the last Yamashita of her generation. She's
fractured her hip, and they've drilled screws into her thighbone. The surgery

is a great success, but the morphine, the IV drip, the catheter, and the stress on her heart knock her out for days. She's down to about eighty-five pounds, a small mound in the bed, and my sister and I sit on either side, waiting, listening to the rhythmic spit of the oxygen machine, the beep and dings of the monitors, the melancholy of some TV soap opera, and a lady named Eleanor two doors down who tries to escape, yelling, *Call security! The doctor is a fake!* I wander into the corridor to check out Eleanor in yellow skid-free socks, her hospital gown with her backside indecently exposed, corralled by nursing personnel. Why not; I'm bored. When the nurses apparently strap Eleanor to the bed, she shouts out repeatedly, *I am bound! I am bound!* Asako can't hear any of this anyway, but we figure the last time Asako was locked up with folks going loony was back in 1942.

I pick up the Benedict and read sections of it out loud to my sister. *Check this out! Japanese are a bundle of contradictions: polite but insolent, rigid but adaptable, submissive but uncontrollable, brave but timid, robotic but insubordinate, western-leaning but conservative, loyal but treacherous, kiku but katana!* I reenact ritual suicide over the book. I wave my wrists around like I could have been a bona fide anthropologist too. *She's not describing Japanese, she's . . .* I gesture toward Asako and burst into laughter.

My sister narrows her eyes. *That's not funny.*

Okay. Okay, I pant, *So Benedict says that Japanese differentiate between obligation and duty. Which is it that we are doing here?*

We stare at the two creases that line Asako's forehead above her nose and between her brows; on a scale of pain, one to ten, it's a seven.

Oh geeze.

Weeks later when Asako emerges from her stupor, I test her long-term memory. *Did you ever read Ruth Benedict's* Chrysanthemum and Sword?

Oh yeah.

So what did you think?

She never went to Japan. Ridiculous. And then they occupied Japan based on that.

I think about this. Japanese internment / Japanese occupation. The WRA camps were like prequels? Minicrucibles? Yikes. If the JAs could maintain their dignity under conditions of great shame and humiliation, why not an entire mother nation? *Oh,* I take a breath. *In the day, did others think like you?*

I don't know. Asako shakes her head.

I press my lips together and attempt a pious look of conjecture. *Well, if Benedict studied the Japanese in camps, maybe she was describing . . . us?* Asako is offended. *We are not Japanese.*

Maybe we are Benedictines. Like you've quoted William Carlos Williams, *the pure products go crazy.* Literally. Meanwhile my cousin Ken e-mails me to let me know that cousin Kix is traveling to Hong Kong to give Sus's grandson a samurai sword that Kix has stored in a locker for a decade. It's not exactly first son to son of first son, but you get the picture. I hope they perform some kind of elaborate exchange ritual. Plus in order to get our family registered as samurai, we have to turn in our family tree with all the birth, death, and marriage dates. I write to my cousin and say that I think the Yamashitas were landed merchants who probably bought sword rights from an impoverished daimyo. No way some old Yamashita died nobly on the battlefield of Sekigahara. But Tomi who only married a Yamashita—she was probably the real thing. I say, *Did you ever see that Tom Cruise movie, The Last Samurai? If it were Tomi, she'd have slit Cruise's skinny white throat.* Like Benedict says General Yamashito [sic] said when the Americans reinvaded the Philippines: *Now the enemy is in our bosom.*

What I get from Benedict is that the reason Japan went to war was for respect. R-E-S-P-E-C-T. And be cognizant of the fact that if you humiliate or shame a Japanese, his *revenge will be virtuous.* I understand this; it is rather like being a fiction writer. And then I relearn from Benedict that the Japanese cultivate the habitual, the pleasurable, and the painful in elaborately artful rituals: drinking tea, sleeping, fornicating, bathing, shooting arrows, playing the violin, wrestling, planting miniature trees, killing, eating, committing suicide. Anyone can learn the habit, which means that it can be predicted, and that unlearning it can also happen. This is the anthropological lesson: social behaviors are patterns. It's just that Japanese patterns are more intricate, trained into efficient thoughtlessness, selflessness, or as they like to say, nuance.

Of all the things I could say about your namesake, I can't resist quoting this passage by Theodora Kroeber:

> *Ishi was orderly by nature probably, and by old habit certainly . . . This easy competence and pleasure in well-ordered arrangements of the tools and possessions of living suggests the Japanese flair for raising mere orderliness to an aesthetic of orderliness. There is a temperamental, and*

possibly a kineaesthetic something in this trait not to be explained by
poverty in the variety of things owned, or difficulty of replacement and
consequent need to take good care of them ... The aesthetic of order and
arrangement would seem to be rather something in-born, deep-seated in
the individual psyche. Some cultures turn this preference and capacity
into an approved value: thus the Yana and the Japanese.

If, like Asako, I live to ninety-eight, I could maybe be the last sansei. House me in any international museum that's a swooping architectural extravaganza, preferably with water and glass and spectacular views and height, and surround me with handlers who invent exotic cocktails and precious gourmet fusion tapas; wash my body and hair in lavender oils; perform the nostalgic and the rude in arts and music. Just make sure I die in sweet sleep, and you can have my brain too.

World Fellowship

Ishi, using your ideas of surrealist juxtapositions, I contemplate here a world war that ended in two atomic bombs, the utter devastation of Japan, and a legacy of atrocities. Then, a Japan that emerges into the Cold War alongside Benedict's reconstitution of feudal practices, practices lifted in part from a Japanese tribe and their descendants who got pickled in segregated communities in the rice vinegar of Meiji Japan and American democracy. All right, I'm overstating the Japanese American role in Benedict's thesis, because I'm amused by the idea that my folks could have been the fodder for a kinder, gentler Zen interpretation of the inscrutable Japanese. What about the industrial revolution, the zaibatsu and yakuza, my grandparents who were encouraged to emigrate to pay rural debts, to colonize a greater Asia, to provide for the national infrastructure as international human bridges? Does it matter that Japan had become modern, required resources to drive its modernity, required military power to assert its right to those resources?

Homer asserts that the idea of God made the modern world possible. The authority of a universal Western god created the possibilities or perhaps the arrogance of discovery and investigation. But it wasn't just the West; the consequences of progress were played out in three Nipponic eras—Meiji, Taisho, Showa—from military and technological prowess to the experiment of nuclear extinction; a people got bombed back into their stone age. What idea of God, even if oriental, was here present? Benedict suggests that what empowered imperial edicts was not belief in the emperor as a living god but belief in rituals of obligation and loyalty. It was the difference between feeling guilty about sin committed against God and feeling shame over one's conduct in God's presence. Homer might say that any idea of God has consequences that are possibly dangerous.

Tomi was proud to be modern and a Christian, and, having sent her two oldest children to be educated in Japan, she must have had hopes for the future. Either she hoped to return to Japan or she believed that her children would truly be a bridge to the West. I wonder if, for Tomi, the idea of a modern world made a Christian god possible. Tomi became converted to Christianity in the United States through her exposure to examples of kindness, but there was also a community built by Japanese Christians in Oakland at the West Tenth Methodist Church. She and other issei women gathered together to found their own kind of social powerhouse. Meiji modernity and emigration gave these women power. You see these widowed ladies posed together in photographs, in pressed Sunday dresses with gloves and hats, gripping their matching purses, and Asako chuckles, *Those ladies ran every-thing. They were a force to contend with.* Japan's gift to an Oakland God.

Tomi's second son Hiroshi was a rascal. At some point, Tomi also gave him the name John. I asked my dad about this, since it was assumed he was named after John the Baptist, but it turns out that Tomi went to the cinema and saw a movie in which a bandit sees the light and is converted to good-ness. Tomi may have felt desperate, but my dad said to me, *I was named after a bandito.* At a young age, he climbed to the top of a fence, jumped off, and broke his hip, the long healing of which kept him in crutches and took him in and out of the Shriner's Hospital for Crippled Children. In one story, Aimee Semple McPherson set up her Pentecostal revival tent some-where in town. Tomi took seven-year-old John to that tent, and he hobbled out without his crutches. Hallelujah, as they say. The doctors were furious, John remembered. *We had to buy new crutches.*

The crutches, the stiff bum leg soldered to the hip, never seemed to stop John, who was known to bat the ball, then scuttle around the bases, likely using his crutches to some defensive advantage. Physical disadvantage never seemed to bother him; he never complained, never made excuses. He knew himself to have a brilliant mind, but I believe his particular bril-liance was his capacity for empathy, the bright reach of his capacious social intelligence.

John was accepted at several institutions: Boston University Theological Seminary, Union Theological Seminary in New York, and Drew Theological School in New Jersey; however, delayed by military and FBI bureaucracy from leaving camp and beleaguered by scarce resources, he would settle for Garrett, the alma mater of his Oakland mentor and protector, Frank Herron Smith, missionary to Japan and Korea and superintendent of the Japanese Metho-dist Mission. Twenty miles north of Chicago on Lake Michigan, Evanston was an upscale and tidy college town known for its strict temperance laws and the Methodists who founded Northwestern University, Garrett Biblical Institute, and five local churches. Arguably, of all the locations John might have landed, it was the most conservative. In the first months after his arrival in Evanston in 1943, John wrote back to the family at Topaz:

I talked to George Matsuyama who ... stated that his camp visit was like a strange dream. Well, with me it's the other way around; this school is yet the dream and my mind keeps wandering back to camp. Whenever I speak to groups and people about the camp I am so intense in my description

that they look at me very curiously . . . at school here they all know
about the camp because of a large FOR group here and sympathetically
express that it's a bad situation and keep giving me cheerful notes; they
always introduce me as one who has just come from an internment camp
and I'm a sort of curio.

Initially he must have felt a responsibility to speak about the camps, and his letters evoke a hectic schedule of speaking engagements, intense coursework, dishwashing, and co-op work to support his studies and dorm residency. By the next year, he retreated into what he justified in his letters as the ivory tower of intellectual solitude; however, I believe that he was silently blacklisted from speaking or offering sermons to the white congregations in the area. His missives to his family seem always upbeat and conscientious, working diligently on his end to create an opening for nisei resettlement into Chicago, but what I sense generally was his absence and psychic solitude. While I cannot say I understand the theological questions of his coursework, I am struck by a lack of intellectual excitement or enthusiasm, the irrelevance of theological questions in the context of war and internment, and the absence of mentorship. I may be wrong about this. John's papers reflect a repeated concern with the validation of faith in the gospel of Jesus's charity and the miracle of his resurrection. If John needed a miracle, so do I. Still, the record of John's presence at Garrett in those years seems to amount to a notation of his divinity degree and that he was a member of the Dempster League, responsible for activities under the heading of *World Fellowship.*

Also curious is the absence of administrative files from the war years in the school's archive. While every other year in Horace Greeley Smith's tenure as president from 1932 to 1953 is meticulously saved, no wartime correspondence from 1941 to 1944 exists. No correspondence from Frank Herron Smith or from John Nason or Joseph Conard representing Nisei Student Relocation; nothing about the surveillance of conscientious objectors, enrolled students eventually arrested by the FBI; and nothing about the community controversy over the lease of Professor Frank McKibben's Evanston home on the corner of Asbury and Noyes.

At the end of February 1944, Chizu and Ed made plans to leave temporary resettlement farm work in Idaho to join brothers John and Tom in Evanston. Edwin Kitow was a Stanford engineering graduate, born in

Japan but having lived since the age of eight in California. He and Chizu had built a profitable produce company in Calexico, in the Imperial Valley at the Mexican frontier. At the outbreak of the war, this business in cantaloupes and lettuce was thriving, but John was the absentee corporate signator of the business since Ed was a Japanese national ineligible for citizenship. Chizu recounted to me that in the prewar they were doing so well that Ed bought her a three-month trip to Japan, a full-length fur coat—useless in Calexico—and a Cadillac, which she drove back and forth across California to visit the family. Chizu was a registered nurse and president of the PTA in Calexico. Unlike others in the salvage, the Kitows probably had means to start a new life in another place. They decided to move to Evanston to be near John. Professor Frank McKibben, who taught at Garrett Seminary, offered to lease his home to the Kitows during his sabbatical. It was an elegant six-bedroom, three-story house that could shelter the three Kitows, bachelor brothers John and Tom, and eventually mother Tomi.

Tom, having graduated the University of Nebraska, had moved to Chicago for an engineering job. He wrote to Kay:

> No luck as far as housing goes. The 6 room flat which was lined up fell through and we went through the same agony again. The owner was willing and so were the immediate neighbors but one of the influential ladies in that district objected and wouldn't even give us a chance to talk to her. She has 4 sons in the South Pacific and threatened to get the rest of the neighborhood aroused . . .

Professor McKibben himself wrote a letter to the editor of a local Evanston newspaper telling a further story—that a neighborhood meeting was convened at the McKibben household and that among those present were Reverend Ernest F. Tittle of the Evanston First Methodist Church; Professor Rockwell Smith, who sponsored John's project, *A Study of a War Relocation Community;* and the President of Garrett Biblical Institute himself, Horace Greeley Smith. McKibben states that, *because of the hostility of the crowd against comment from those outside the neighborhood,* these prominent men did not speak. If you visit the neighborhood, you realize that Garrett Seminary is only blocks from this house, that it is indeed within the neighborhood and part of its community, and you wonder also that a local minister to that same neighborhood could not speak, as McKibben suggests, *in opposition to any doctrine of racial superiority* and in support of *the real meaning of the Four Freedoms.*

This is an event I heard retold by the family on numerous occasions. It marks, I believe, the end of any naïve relationship to a liberal church and reveals the environment of John's invisibility during those years. I have not had to create a fiction here to retell this story. If you google the other names in McKibben's letter, their prestige and scholarship, especially as Far East Asian pundits and missionaries, bubble to the screen. Did they not have a moral responsibility as religious leaders and missionaries? Their silence may have been golden or *tactful* as perhaps the frustrated McKibbon makes their apology, but as anthropologist Benedict advises regarding shaming a Japanese, my revenge will be *virtuous.*

In order to accelerate his graduation from Garrett, John took courses during the summer months. By February 14, 1945, he was on a train, *en route Coach Challenger,* back to visit the almost defunct camp Topaz, then on to Oakland to reopen the Oakland West Tenth Church. Arriving six months before the official end of the war, he must have been among the first Japanese Americans to return home. Appearing like an apparition on Oakland streets, he ducked into the old church to receive his violent welcome home: the crack of gunshots, ricochet of bullets. This story about gunshots might be apocryphal; it wasn't one of those stories repeated like family lore. I heard it from my sister who remembers hearing it only once from John. *You know Dad,* she said. *Said he was shot at and then laughed.* No big deal. Even thirty years after the war, still holding responsibility for the character of his role as upbeat and steady counselor, John would seek to suppress the negative and sensational.

The church had been filled with the left-behind belongings of evacuees, boarded shut during the war, and assiduously guarded by a friend of the church, Lee Mullis, and his father. John began acquiring cots and blankets and turned the church into a hostel to receive the residue of returning folks, many now homeless, all fearful and skeptical about their future. Despite the pained and angry resentment of the returnees, John kept seriously on task and was mostly joyous. Indeed, in his train letter approaching Cheyenne, John advised Kay to

> *feel independent and seek the situation which makes for the most peaceful now and in regards to the future . . . be ready to take off where your heart calls and interests lie. Don't let circumstances shape your affairs*

too much . . . In the change learned much and saw more. I maintain in America we have a women's world—They have the initiative to make up men's minds for them . . . I say all is adventure and more adventure and if you don't want it—then don't venture forth in faith, but be content with things as they are . . . Here's to you for new worlds to be.

John

Here then was the incorrigible and cheerful romantic who refused to be diminished by the war, by any idea of salvage or shame, who returned home to push open old church doors, to sort through and put to new use the stored artifacts of lives left behind.

Lease to Jap-Americans Ended; Dr. McKibben Makes Statement

Editor, EVANSTON REVIEW: Inasmuch as an article appeared in THE REVIEW concerning our attempt to rent our home at 2231 Asbury avenue to Japanese-American people it seems only fair that we be permitted to make a more adequate and correct statement of the situation and of our reasons for this action.

After talking with one of our neighbors who was certainly not very enthusiastic about such rental but who raised no fundamental objection, we leased our home to this Japanese-American family. Soon, however, objections began to come in and some of our neighbors began ringing doorbells up and down our street and adjacent streets. We realized that something should be done. We invited our near neighbors to our home for a friendly conference. Practically the entire neighborhood came. We have held all kinds of meetings in our home, but this was the first time we invited our neighbors to come in and hold a protest meeting against us! It was a spirited but fairly friendly meeting.

Wife Is Native of U. S.

Comment was made to the effect that we should rent our home to Americans. Of course, that is exactly what we proposed to do. We rented to a Mrs. Dorothy Kitow, an American of Japanese descent, born in America, trained in its culture, and a graduate of one of its universities, the University of California. It happens that her husband was born in Japan, coming to this country at the age of 8, and growing up in this country, prevented by law from becoming a citizen. He studied engineering at Leland Stanford university, and was engaged in farming in California when the war broke out. The Kitows owned their own home from which they were ejected upon 24 hours' notice. He was a member of the Rotary club of his community and they are both active Protestants. They are a refined, educated couple with a 9-year-old son.

Encounter Opposition

In attempting to give these people a home we thought we were doing an American and Christian thing. They, and people like them, are having a desperately difficult time finding housing. We would be glad to have them in our home and would ourselves certainly welcome them as neighbors.

It seemed to us also that such action was thoroughly in harmony with the avowed aims of our present war; namely, opposition to any doctrine of racial superiority such as the Nazis are promulgating. Such vigorous opposition as we encountered makes us wonder what we are fighting for anyway, and what is the real meaning of the Four Freedoms. We were much disturbed over some of the speeches made at our home. As one of our neighbors who was at the meeting wrote us the next day, "I actually wept to think that the two lads of our family have already given a year's service and may be called upon to give their lives for such mouthings of Christian and democratic principles."

Kitows Surrender Lease

The Kitows upon being informed of the situation, immediately offered to surrender the lease, as we expected they would, not desiring to live under such conditions. Nor would we want them to do so.

And so ends the matter. Or does it? This matter is of much greater proportions than just that of neighbors and real estate values. It raises the question of what Evanstonians believe in and are willing to fight for.

Among those present Monday night but who did not speak because of the hostility of the crowd against comment from those outside the neighborhood were: Dr. E. F. Tittle, Dr. Emory Luccock, Dr. Harrison Franklin Rall, Dr. and Mrs. Harold Ruopp, Mr. and Mrs. Rockwell Smith, and Dr. H. G. Smith, who was asked to serve as moderator of the meeting. Dr. Roy Smith of the Chicago Church federation, who was in Tokyo for six months after Pearl Harbor, was also present and spoke on behalf of the Kitows. Albert Moon was present representing the War Relocation authority.

Sincerely yours,
Frank M. McKibben

1925

Dear Ishi:

I suppose I could have named you Margaret Mead or even Ruth Benedict, but I wanted a connection, like Homer, to deep storytelling. As you warn, I may be taken to task for this blasphemy, but as we are told, *Ishi* was not really the name of the last Yahi in California; it was the name he accepted in his new life as artifact or perhaps in the sense of John's being a *curio* out of camp, the old life lost forever.

You appreciate the idea that forced internment coupled with the anthropological framing of wartime studies conspired to create the social conditions for the collective psyche of a people who, forced to perform loyalty, assimilation, and modeled-ness, became *loyal* and *assimilated* and *modeled* in order to survive. But, very perceptively, you also ask about refusal and resistance, what people kept for themselves in order not to change, to maintain independence, or to refuse outright, those declaring no-no and renouncing American citizenship. This outright refusal is a longer and very crucial history that cannot be contained in this project, but the substance of resistance is perhaps what I am attempting here to draw out or at least to complicate. As our story goes, the Yamashita family closed ranks under a united banner of yes-yes, but the two eldest siblings, Susumu and Kimi, were kibei, educated and raised in Japan. Sus in particular worked for Mitsubishi and was likely always under surveillance. Sus's allegiances were no doubt divided, but as the eldest son and head of family, he was in no position to resist. With the notice for evacuation, the extended family moved into his home in Oakland in order to be evacuated together. Chiz and Ed with their young son Kix drove across California from Calexico to crowd into that small house. What Sus felt, he kept to himself, but the story is that at war's end, Sus shaved away his thin mustache as, perhaps, a small sign to himself.

You take umbrage with my desire for *virtuous* revenge over the failure of church elders in Evanston to support the short-term rental of Professor McKibben's house to Chiz and Ed. I admit I do not believe in revenge as virtuous in the sense of honorably justified; I am only needling Benedict. But perhaps it's possible to word-play with the virtuosity of justice, a desire for fluency and change of heart. You read the McKibben letter as very fair, that silence in this case would have been *tactful,* and you question what outsiders could have done in this situation. You feel my critique of liberal Christianity needs unpacking and complication. Frank McKibben's letter, I too believe, was fair and measured, and McKibben himself is a small hero in this story, but why would he have named the outside persons who came to moderate or to witness this meeting? For me, naming these illustrious men was to call attention to their presence and their fear. But there is also the family—Chizu who kept this yellowed newspaper clipping all these years and Kix, her son, who saved it as well. I feel it is fair to report the oral storytelling that became a part of the family outrage and served as a backdrop to John's sadness and muddled scholarship in Evanston. But it is also for this reason that Caleb Foote and the Quakers are a part of this story, because they refused to be silenced. And that perhaps is my larger question: Why?

Sincerely yours,

LETTERS TO
Love

Dear Vyasa:

One day, I received a telephone call from you. In those years, I was working at the television station; how did you find me in those dark ages before cyber? Perhaps you wrote to me through my publisher, and appropriately we corresponded. You were editing a book about Asians in the Americas. Would I contribute something about Japanese in Brazil? I was amazed and gratified. You were among a half-dozen American scholars interested in the subject, but unlike the specificity of most academic scholarship, you were expansive in your reach, casting your net across the entire hemisphere, across any genre of cultural production that could be represented in a book, and encompassing the diaspora from the broadest possible geography that might define Asia, from Lebanon to Japan. In one book, you reclaimed the halving of the world—north and south, old and new, occident and orient, first and third—by twisting the globe in a crisscross of human migrations. Your vision was expansive in your desire for inclusion—amateur and professional, academic and layperson, matured and youthful—all would be given voice. I realize that is why we met; you sought me out on a hunch, that some obscure writer hidden in the engineering department of a television station might have something to say.

It must have been years later that we actually met face-to-face for Chinese lunch. You invited another guest, a Chinese American scholar. None of us had ever met. You arranged what you call a contrapuntal meeting to create a beginning of some possibility. Three American women from multiple diasporas—Chinese, South Asian, Japanese—met over tea and tofu and created a new space of knowing. This day stays in your memory because, as you confessed later, you went home with an MSG attack. You might have been tricked by the sensation of dying, but if it's any consolation, memorable for me was learning to value the surprise of the contrapuntal.

It took me many years from that first meeting to get to know your traveling body and its traveling memories. You were born in Bombay, raised in Karachi, educated in Beirut, Durham, and Berkeley, and adopted by a second family in Oaxaca. And by complicated routes that I have no doubt confused, your great-great-grandmother was Chinese from Shanghai, your great-grandfather born in China, and your mother in Yokohama. You speak Hindi, Gujarati, Urdu, English, Spanish, and read Sanskrit and Greek. One day you explained how, in the seventh century CE, the Persian Sassanid Empire was replaced by the Arab, and thus the Zoroastrian by the Islamic, which heralded the exodus and diaspora of your people. Pondering this starting place, I asked if your folks ever thought of returning to claim Iran as a homeland. Your response was angry and adamant: *Absolutely not!* I was taken aback by the fierceness in your voice. It was only later that I understood, not that I had asked a stupid question, but that the idea of a national home is antithetical to everything you believe. You would teach me that there are dreams and memories that make human creation possible, but to dream the memory of home might be the most dangerous. *It is,* you have insisted, *not always where you were born that makes you who you are.*

Your letters are so full —
I wish you would write —

You speak of creative growth —
the theocentric way —

This implies a definition of man's potential — about
which I do not know — ?
I'll read Nygren?

Only this I would like to ask — in your emphasis upon [...]
flowing — do you imply that no suffering is ever destructive?
It seems to me that [...]ve or [...] or [...] for
[...] ignores life — that the conflicts setting up are apt to [...]
[...] totality of [...] — men can [...]
[...] flames some values and truths to which they were able to [...]

Your comments on education — I would like to [...]
[...] time this time — I want to
[...] time to — but just superficially [...]
[...] all you say is probably at least partially true — and some [...]
[...]pletely true — but you oversimplify so called — liberal [...]
[...] Thinking of it as a 'sheltering process' — and I do what I like to do [...]
It seems to me that education has always tended to [...]

Why are you doing this?

[...]ltering and stieting growth.
Only the few formerly arrived — they arrived
[...] to be sure — but more often by complete conformity to a rigid [...]
were the [...] disciplined, trained and stamped. Linguistically th[...]
[...]ed. What about inner, creative growth? — It was incidental — Life [...]
[...]plies persuaded or didn't — and so it was — a survival of what? —
[...] about the rest? — the big average — and the slightly under average —
[...] stunts of them? — Have they a capacity for growth? — how do they grow [...]
[...] as you said — "through a fine precarious balance of paint [...] trial
[...] practice" — Even if we would, we could not shelter this man [...]
[...] schools against life's processes — but we do try to [...]
[...] on their level, conducive to growth [...]

71

Toward the end of February 1945, John Yamashita stepped off a train at the Oakland depot, returning home after three years' absence. Meanwhile Alma Gloeckler had been teaching in the Oakland public schools and had spent the previous summer at Tule Lake Segregation Center. She was at Tule Lake in Christmas 1944, when the closing of camps was announced. As John's train approached, Alma, a lone stranger, showed up to meet him at the depot. She wrote:

> I can still see John, standing at the Oakland train depot with a small luggage, as I got out of my little black depression Chevy. He was serious. We greeted one another formally and introduced ourselves . . . I told him that Josephine Duveneck of AFSC had informed me of his arrival. John was just a little less serious, and seemed reassured. "Why are you doing this?" he asked right away. That remained a short question and a long time to answering.

Alma accompanied John to the West Tenth Japanese Methodist Church to begin the work of reopening its doors as a hostel to receive returning Japanese Americans and to distribute the stored belongings—furniture, mattresses, stoves, refrigerators, sewing machines—left behind by some 135 families. Alma gave John that *black depression* Chevy to pick up returnees and supplies, and daily she and a cohort of what she called *settled people* came to scrub, clean, and paint the church's Meader Hall. Old cots used in camp were redeployed, blankets gathered, and Alma's friend Bernice Cofer organized Lakeshore Avenue Baptist church members to stand in ration lines at Capwell's to buy sheets and pillowcases, two to a customer. Margaret Utsumi and John's old Berkeley schoolmate Ish Isokawa returned as those eventually *settled people*—Margaret to set up the kitchen and dining service and Ish to work long hours at John's side, shipping trunks and crated boxes of belongings to those who'd never return. Many years later, John would write to Ish: *You know I've never really thanked you for that year back in '45 when you ran the Hostel and emptied out West Tenth Gym . . .* John got a small stipend from the Methodist Youth Fellowship, but Ish and Margaret worked those years without pay. In the next year and a half, three thousand people would pass through the church into relocated and recuperated lives. In this busy churning of folks there was little time to thank anyone, but perhaps also little will to show gratitude. Mean years had turned people mean; that is also to say terse, speechless, socially closed and, as you can imagine, afraid and mistrusting.

Alma's memories emphasized John's careful protection of the hostel's *feeling climate,* protective of the feelings of the returnees as much as of those who offered succor to them. John wanted something back, an emotional generosity that fulfilled his beliefs. He cultivated, Alma described, a *heightened awareness* that *met every person and every contingency.* While Alma understood that hostilities had to be *thawed out,* she was impatient with public ignorance and continuing negative attitudes toward the returning Japanese and said so. She remembered John's reaction: *John listened thoughtfully, head down, and then said softly . . . "Don't make any enemies for yourself, on account of us."*

Perhaps John was already aware of the disturbed feelings of Lee Mullis who had, with his father Fred, watched over and protected Meader Hall and its contents during the war years. This must have meant constant vigilance against certain vandalism, checking it at night, repairing and boarding up broken windows. It must have also meant incurring the wrath and abuse of neighbors, losing friends, becoming over time isolated and worn with responsibility. Lee Mullis, the only Caucasian member of a Japanese church, had said good-bye to friends and their fellowship, and for that, had taken on an almost impossible promise, the burden of obligation. Miraculously, he kept his promise while so many encumbered others had not, abandoning or selling what was not theirs. When the war ended and relief seemed in sight, Lee opened the church and hoped to welcome home his friends. Who he welcomed home were an unsettled and broken people, refugees in their own country, returned to lives forever changed, psychically contained by a thin veneer of politeness that for many years would hide deep fear, suspicion, and pained resentment. If no one thanked Ish for the next thirty years, indeed, no one thought of thanking Lee and his father. Old friends never returned, never sent word, or sent for their stuff with a few lines in a telegram. Other friends returned, stayed provisionally at the hostel, and silently left.

In John's *Pastor's Record of Funerals,* the first recorded funeral at Oakland West Tenth was that of Fred Thomas Mullis on January 12, 1946. The *Oakland Tribune's* obituary section read

Death: Mullis—in Clear Lake woodlands, January 7, 1946. Fred Thomas Mullis, husband of the late Fannie K. Mullis, father of Loren Lee Mullis, Mrs. B. W. Payne, and the late Mrs. E. H. Hawkins. A native of Kansas, aged 70 years, 2 months, 21 days. Friends are invited to attend the services

at the Japanese M. E. Church. 10th and West Street, Oakland, Saturday, January 12, 1946 at 2 o'clock p.m.

John presided over the funeral and burial, but who among the original congregation at West Tenth joined Lee Mullis in mourning his father? A sad absence surrounds this event, the details of which have been entirely lost. Some time after his father's death, Lee also left Oakland without word, headed to New York, never to be thanked and never to be heard from again.

In another two years, Alma, too, would leave for New York to pursue a graduate degree in education at Columbia. I'm not sure that Alma and John ever met again. It was many years later that I finally met Alma Gloeckler. At the age of one hundred, she remarked with amused disdain that *age is not a disease,* although dementia is, and Alma to the very end had almost every marble in place. Her hair coiled up in an elegant French braid, Alma looked at me with bright curious eyes, and I knew she searched for and saw her old friend John, that he somehow appeared between us and lived in our moments together, her remembering and storytelling. John saved three letters from Alma that he himself dated around 1946; reading them, after reading all his seminary papers written during the war, finally I sensed what had been absent in his seminary work: a kindred spiritual and intellectual partnership. The letters wander, but with thoughtfulness and spiritual inquisition, a sense of pleasure in thinking a thought through without recrimination, but with expectation and surprise. Though John's corresponding letters are lost, this insight remains. For John, 1945 to 1947 were years of intense physical and emotional work, the practical labor of rebuilding a postwar community, but it was also a period of intense personal, political, and philosophical questioning. Alma's correspondence makes it clear that the labor of the period—practical and philosophical— would be the underpinning of John and Alma's understanding about civil society and civil rights.

The questions implied in the letters are philosophically enormous and uncontainable. They boggle and pain the mind. *Why and how should one choose a spiritual path? What is the church? How does one cultivate a conscience? How do we know we know? Is belief logical? What is prayer? What is confession? What about the simplicity of a life lived daily without question? What is suffering? Sacrifice? Giving? What is education? Creativity? What are the laws of nature, and what is human freedom? What is the meaning and danger of giving and receiving? What is love?* Alma and John together began with the assumption of a spiritual center and caring social conduct, Alma influenced by her Canadian Mennonite family and cultivated through Quaker membership, and John, being the son of Japanese immigrants and a student of Rollo May, Reinhold Niebuhr, and Howard Thurman.

Among these heady inquiries, I am drawn to Alma's conscientious struggle with her fluctuating position as giver and receiver, her understanding of the uneven power and privilege of the giver. She wrote

It seems that if we are going to deal affectively with one another, helpfully and with understanding and strength—we need to know something more about just what that relationship between giver and receiver can be at best. Love itself is a wonderful enlightener because it adds patience and kindliness—hope and faith to a relationship, but it too needs all the enlightenment it can get in a complicated conflicting social order. So back I am at the question of self—to lose it and yet to find it—more viably. I do think that we must realize that at best it involves repeated failures even in the realm of giving—suffering and a feeling of futility at times . . .

John asked Alma: *Why are you doing this?* It was not, as Alma knew, a simple question. Perhaps it was a forewarning. Homer would say that the nature of true charity is much like taxes, an understanding that this is how a civil society is paid for. Charity must be its own reward. But what about love? Perhaps Lee Mullis held forth with the expectation of love and family, but he got stuck at home with all the old stuff that, finally preserved and saved, did not really matter. How could he know? It's difficult to think clearly ahead about why you might do anything—why take on love, why risk heartbreak? The only other thing I've been able to learn about Lee Mullis is that he died at the age of eighty-two in Glen Cove, Nassau, on Long Island, in 1987. Forty years lived after the war, although the resilience of bitterness is unpredictable; hopefully, as John and Alma would have wished, love intervened.

DAD.   Mullis

FUNERAL ORDER OF WORSHIP
JAN. 12th, 1945 —

INVOCATION: (Let us pray)

VIOLIN SOLO. — (favorite hymn)

SCRIPTURES: Psalms 23, John 14:1-6, Rev. 14:13

PIANO SOLO.

WORDS BY THE MINISTER

CLOSING PRAYER:

O God, the Lord of life, the Conqueror of death,
our help in every time of trouble, who dost not
willingly grieve or afflict the children of men;
comfort us who mourn, and give us grace, in the
presence of death, to worship thee, that we may
have sure hope of eternal life and be enabled to
put our whole trust in thy goodness and mercy;

Here, then, we commit to Thine unfailing love the
beloved soul now departed. We thank Thee for the
gracious memories which gather about this life, for
kindly deeds and thots, for the love freely given
and the love modestly received, and now at last for
quiet release from the burden of the flesh and
entrance into the peace reserved for those who love
Thee. The Lord gave, and the Lord hath taken away;

The West Tenth Methodist Church

769-797 TENTH STREET -:- OAKLAND 7, CALIFORNIA

Telephone GLencourt 1-3519

Nov. 13, 1947

Kay,

T hanks for your expressive letter and I want to answer it right now my thots move fast in my reaction to it. I just got back from my regular day morning golf date which I have not missed unless I could help it for the year and it gives me the weekly exercise and sunshine. We are all very well he weather, food and shelter is as it should be here so good that we cannot very thankful; mother is quite well in morale too. She hopes to trek out at the beginning of the new year when I hope things go on schedule and I sha ttled. She keeps thoroughly occupied with our program here and packages for with things and thots of you in between.

Let me say first that I like the way you put your thots down just as you tly feel them for it gives me a clear live of your mood and state of mind. people cannot express themselves, their best friends are in the dark and at to establish rapport. Your work as I see it from your letter is entirely co tive and adventure... experiences as you g at score I can se... not... rather are unconsciously gro every new contact you make and every new personality you meet, as well as th us environments you make yourself at home in. I think in the end you will f bit of it a good and valuable memory and part of accumulated wisdom. That I envy you; if you... without getting too careerish in t in a sense of being too worldly-wise and tired because you've seen a lot. it all in as stored-up experience which adventure keeps you fresh and with a ok 'of a twinkle in your eye"; well, that's to use all of these days of your rich future. I see so many people, who are at a loss for conversation beca see little, read less and cannot take advantage of every new day as a refres nteresting experience. It's sad when there are so many things to probe, imp hich in turn make for our steady (and often unconscious growth). So I don't your work, rather I see you are really to be envied in the challenging e of the job of your organization. I think if one takes it as such, and not which means a wage, one may find that the work in all of its aspects can be ed very lightly and bring refreshment in rewards. Never drive yourself too m job- it tires you and shows up in a stale morale which is most damaging and immediately by those whose support you would solicit and those you would enc ganization thus in the longrun benefits by the overwork or overdrive of its rs. This theme- I presume I've stated lately to Tom -& I state it thusly to

Regards Mech- let me say -you are right to a great extent. Let me give alysis: Like all males he pursued an idea and we do that (so often without or the right enthusiasm because we think that's where we should move for we new or other incentive). A gal senses anything short of a sweep-youeoff-the ach and as a gal she doesn't warm up to it instinctively. If the gal is old ther blockings or barriers in her mind - she of course warms up to it less egree that she ponders and debates. The male in the meantime (altho his app olid and clumsy, is, at heart romantic) and he knows and of course is hurt in e none-response; but he pursues because of his pride and wants to make a con because his move represents a challenge. However, at the moment he finds th has finished her pondering and has calculated that the guy is a good catch - t the moment he senses the gal might be won- has satisfied his challenge and urt pride -but the cool calculation has iced his ardor -and he becomes at th t the -ponderer and calculator; at this point, he begins to doubt everything e gal was doubting his ardor-less attention.

Come live with me in poverty

79

Vyasa, you have said that truth is not the fact of history or a story's memory but its accountability. What then are these letters? Being written on a certain day and near or at the time of the events, are they less unstable and closer to being true? Or are events, written about in contemplation after they have occurred, more true? There are John and Alma's letters written in their mid-thirties, and then there are those written in old age in precarious handwriting, the mind grasping for clarity, privileging simplicity. Here I am plunged close to the hearts of my folks, the raw stuff, and yet despite the immediacy, so much has gone unexpressed, flowing away under that bridge. Now we meet at this temporal distance, and all is speculation. There are letters without corresponding replies. There are gaps between paragraphs and sentences. Someone left writing to brew a cup of coffee, to answer the phone, to leave that thought for another day. There is thinking without continuity, history without continuity, but if continuity could be reconstructed, what would be recuperated? Pressed against the evidence of real penned letters, I am wary of my propensity for dishonesty or, as you say more kindly, fictionalizing. And I have become weary of continuity's plodding plot. I long for a bounding, energetic leap to knowledge, as if wisdom should appear with age. I, too, grasp for clarity and simplicity, the simple truth. You shake your head.

On December 4, 1946, John wrote to sister Kay that he'd taken his brother Tom's gift of two *Big Game* Cal/Stanford tickets for *a foursome* with Ish and Osa Isokawa, and Asako Sakai.

> *The game was very bad, but date was rather nice. She seems to know you pretty well—Very neat unobtrusive person—congenial—and of course college girl. Have seen also 2 plays with the Party—"Glass Menagerie" and "State of the Union"—popular productions so I caught up on the theatre and I'm not sure how much more. I'd be interested in your reactions.*

This note was followed a week later by a second letter to Kay, a long, rambling, four-page, single-spaced typewritten letter, pontificating on the nature of love. While Kay kept carbon copies of every letter she wrote to the family during the camp years, much of her letter writing in the postwar has disappeared. The lost letter Kay wrote to John, encouraging his long response, likely related her college relationship to Asako at Cal Berkeley and her opinion about John's romantic interest. Kay's letters must have also voiced her discouragement with her own prospects of marriage, and, upon the closing of the wartime services of nisei student relocation, a sense of loss of purpose or relevance in her life's work, along with the hardship in finding and relocating to a new job.

From that distance, John's letters to Kay are a funny mixture of brother, counselor, and confessor, giving counsel based on the confessions of his own experience. And this is further complicated by his romantic, philosophical, and religious thinking, by which he justified his living practice and still thought to give encouragement to Kay.

> *Since writing you I have been very sure of my mind . . . I am quite impulsive and hardly rational when it comes to my likes . . . I hold to this because I believe one's prejudices should be basically emotional . . . I don't care for understanding that is not immediate and uncalculated . . . This which is termed FAITH enters largely into my picture, and I have a notion it is the dimension which should enter more widely into every and all adventures of matrimonial designs . . . Well, the short of all of this—is, I like the gal a lot . . .*

John further confessed his difficulty in having a romantic interest while also running a church.

> *. . . I sure have had to devise ways and means to develop my private interest. Boy, never get into a spot like I am (that is, having a Church, supposed degree, and being a Protestant most normally should be married to do the best work). You can't pursue your personal interest without being tabbed as a flighty playboy; and just how can you be charming without being free . . .*

But then John returned to his general pontification on love, eros woven with agape, or as you'd point out from Sanskrit, *kama* with *sneha*, reading like a run-on rendition of Khalil Gibran speaking Corinthians.

> *I do not think you have the right apprehension of that which is Love or that which should be Love. True love never regrets, it's given without a price, it doesn't think in terms of returns, it doesn't expect to be understood, it tries to understand; true love is extravagant, it overflows and if unreciprocated it only seeks the fulfillment not of one's own desire but of the one it concerns. Thus, it respects the other's choice, the other's lack of*

*choice, the other's humor or lack of humor, the other's lack of industry or
ardor—whatever it is—it respects. When people mourn—or they have
too many regrets—I take it that their love was closer to infatuation—to
self-love and geared to the ego, because it is the tearing of the ego which
they feel the pain of—and they do not feel thankful for the pain of knowing love.*

John wanted Kay to lose herself to the plunge, but he probably also wanted
Asako to do the same.

*I say this . . . love freely, love extravagantly, love unreservedly but give your
whole heart and being everything—or it isn't worth giving—and you
insult the receiver . . . to love without being loved, to love without concern
of return, to love because it's good to love—that's worth more—infinitely
more. I say to a woman if you want to be worth your weight in gold—love
first and love in the faith that it is love which will resolve all shortcomings,
prejudices, and circumstances whether in the lover or the loved and this
will lead to growing adventures. It is this sort of love which spurs a man
to believe that he can remove mountains, that makes him change, that
makes him understand there is something else worth building for.*

Okay, Dad. The story that we heard again and again was that some time
after the *Big Game* and maybe two more theater dates later, John proposed
to Asako, and for the next twelve months, Asako kept John's ring without
making a decision. So the letters between John and Kay continue on for
months with comments such as, *one can never know how a woman's mind
really works—I shall not try to identify its reasons any more,* or more urgently,

*I need good advice now not later. The gal took ill with flu and I won't see
her for a couple of weeks. There seems to be a great mental or spiritual
conflict—and I've decided to back away—because I sure wouldn't want
anything on the basis of being just a good guy—My paths are going to be
too rough for any uncertain compromises or sentiments. One can never
trade a soul for a bit of pottage.*

Sprinkled into John's letters were the haiku of Rabindranath Tagore,
but by May of 1947 he was quoting George Bernard Shaw and Plato, while
still preaching about great philosophical and idealistic, yet down-to-earth,

love. Plus, he had a series of recommendations of bachelor men for Kay to meet, and in the background of the letters was the constant reference to "B," Kay's ex from college who never seemed to disappear. Poor Kay, with her literally fluttering heart and graying hair. As the years passed, John referred to Kay as his *spinster sister,* as if he'd escaped becoming a spinster brother, but Asako remembered: *Kay and I ate lunch together at Cal every day, and all she ever talked about was Bobby. Bobby this and Bobby that. She held a torch for him.* As for John's pursuit of *a chain and a ball,* by June, the entire project seems to have gone sour.

> *Yesterday I finally pressed the point why she did not wear my ring and she wouldn't explain again (over 3 months) and wanted to call everything off. I decided that was for the best for she can't see her way clear—she is close-mouthed and finally told me without reasonable information that it was impossible . . . I have no regrets—I gain wisdom . . .*

And as to Kay's apparent moaning and indecision about the men in her life, he responded with irritation, *Kay, clear your cobwebs away,* and chafes at Kay's sentimental cliché about the *coming someday of a beautiful dawn,* retorting that *that will be when, one foot in the grave, you suddenly find wisdom . . . I don't intend to wait that long.*

Then, suddenly in November, John's golf game improved; he reports *technically breaking 90* and

> *just the other day—I find the gal—as cool as a cucumber—put my ring on—say she is giving up smoking—and when I told her that I told my supt. that I really wanted to get married at the first of year and him to perform the ceremony—she said "Let's plan on that." Well, that was also the first evening that she ate like a horse, and talked of everything just as she felt it and as things came to her mind, and she then went to sleep on my shoulder on the way home. That night—I was the speechless—stuttering guy—because the sudden change of affairs caught me unprepared and all my persuasive designing words were unnecessary and irrelevant . . . all of a sudden I put on all the brakes—and had a scared sense of responsibility; because as you know—I have inferiority complexes—regards stature, money, and general kind providing-ways regards those whose love I take for granted; and immediately I've been dogged with a question "can I make her fully happy in the way she might*

expect it"—because my life and vocation is no picnic or bed of roses . . .
Mating love is a most interesting game. Let me tell you: when a gal decides
decisively and with all her heart and soul—for an unknown future—
that's what makes a guy humble and it will give him an incentive to climb
the stars—to justify her faith.

There remain no letters to or from Asako, though I try to imagine they existed. I can't believe John didn't write the same long-winded stuff to Asako, but maybe he knew better. If he did write, those letters were long ago destroyed; Asako had no interest or nostalgia in keeping records or memorabilia. She was *unobtrusive,* unpretentious, and reserved. John was the storyteller, garrulous, funny, and always entertaining. When John retold the story of their year long precarious engagement, usually over dinner with guests and strangers, Asako always pressed her lips together tightly and suppressed embarrassed laughter. She never protested or told her side of the story. The story was about John's pursuit, disappointment, and love, but also about Asako's reticence and what seemed over the years to solidify into their opposing personalities: spontaneous and constrained, idealist and pragmatist, romantic and realist. It was a story with its own sort of truth, the bonding of two sides of a coin, the merging of a couple whose differences would finally care for the other and accomplish that adventure of growth, almost as John's theory of love had predicted. I wouldn't say it was easy. In fact, it never quite made sense to me, except that one always thought to bring the surprise of the rose bouquet and the other remembered to pick the flowers and to pay for it.

Years after John died, and just before her eighty-eighth birthday, I asked Asako about this old story. *What was that story about keeping Dad's ring for an entire year?*

Asako looked at me indignantly. She would finally have the last word. *Do you know how he proposed to me? This is what he said: "Come live with me in poverty."*

...d Thurman on the Sunday following Mahatma Gandhi's death.

Mahatma Gandhi has influenced more human beings directly perhaps anyone else in our time.

...eath makes us go through bureau drawers for old manuscrip... ...n is always a Refreshur Course in the meaning of life.

...hen Dr. and Mrs. Thurman went to India on the Christian ...dship Pilgrimage (with another Negro couple) at the invitat... ...Indein college students, Mr. Gandhi invited them to spend t... ...stmas holidays at his ashram. Low blood pressure did not pe... ...his receiving them, or at New Delhi, later.

One morning, 2 weeks before sailing, H. T. awoke one mornin... ...ing the urgency to wire Mr. Gandhi for an interview. As he ...ted for the telegraph office, one of Gandhi's followers appr... ...ched him with a letter, saying that Gandhi was 4 hours from... ...ay, that they were expected. But if their schedule was too ...clad, he could come to Bombay, that he and the delegation... ...some thing...

The Thurmans and Carroll... ...that same evening ...rain, were met at 5:00 a.m. by Mr. Gandhi's secretary in an... ...Model-T Ford. From then until daybreak Sue slept in a bun... ...w tent (5 rooms) and Howard sat under a .....tree and talked... ...he Secretary about Gandhi.

Upon arrival at Bardoli, the Indian National Congress flag... ...seen. Mr. Gandhi came to the car to greet them. He gave... ...a hand out of the car. He offered to get 2 chairs from a... ...r down the road, if.........

...taking an old-fashioned silver-plated watch out, he said... ...since there was only a period of 3... hours available, and... ...e was so much to talk about, it must be done "by the watch". ...uestioned them for three hours.

Saying that they must have some questions to ask him, he ...asked a favor: Would they sing a spiritual? Would they... ..., "Were you there when they crucified my Lord?". He said... ...t this spiritual was "one of the great, timeless insights of... ...gion".

Howard Thurman said to us, "Needless to say, it was DONE LOVE".

Then Howard's questions: Why had non-violence campaign... ...ed of its objective? Answer: A great ideal, to be effective... ...a period of adequate duration, must become the personal... ...ession of the great mass of people. The Indian mass do... ...have the vitality, for they are hungry (millions have been... ...a lifetime). "I withdrew from politics & began the work of... ...spinning wheel, for it could provide a link between physical... ...ngth and moral vitality."

The greatest drawback was a lack of self-respect, not becaus... ...he British but because of untouchability. Contempt of anoth... ...injury to the soul. So.... Gandhi adopted an untouchable... ...(became an intimate part of the household); changed the na... ...ouchable" (pariah) to a word meaning "child of God". "For if... ...ste Hindu calls this name, the constant repetition will crea... ...sense in the spirit of the Hindu."

A moral frustration will thereby be set up, until the perso... ...ges his attitude to fit the term. (This with a half-chuckle... ...only weapon I know is the spirit of truth". Within 15 mon... ...province had opened all Hindu temples to this caste.

Vyasa, you would have preferred reference to the *Ramayana,* but like the *Iliad,* the *Mahabharata* is about war, and sadly it is war and its aftermath that here haunts my family. What can an ancient epic about war and, furthermore, civil war and fratricide, say about a modern war? Well, first of all, you will remind me that no killing war is civil and that all wars are between brothers. Like the Trojan War, in the end, the battlefield is strewn with the dead bodies of heroes and presumably everyone else who came to get a bit role in the epic, all one hundred Kaurava brothers plus one defecting Pandava brother and all the born and unborn progeny of the Pandavas. On the one side, no Kaurava is left to rule, and on the other, no future Pandava. In eighteen days, six million people die. It doesn't matter if the Pandava brothers are all, like Achilles, the biological (if that's possible) sons of gods, or if their grandfather is the poet telling the story. *Excuse me just one moment while I stop the narrative to have sex with two of my beautiful female characters. Oh, that felt good.* But during sex with the old poet, this sister cringes her eyes shut, and that sister, though wide-eyed, turns deathly pale. The resulting sons cannot be perfect: Dhritarashtra, father of the Kauravas, is born blind; Pandu, father of the Pandavas, is born white and—okay this is confusing— impotent. Let that be a lesson; never insult the author. Or perhaps it does matter that it is the poet's story to tell, that it is the poet's progeny whose great gifts and great faults sow this tale of greed, exile, and destruction, and therefore the poet's responsibility is to offer wisdom in exchange.

Oh but what wisdom, you shake your head. What was the scribe Ganesha thinking, dipping his great tusk into ink and scribbling this tome. Parts of this read like the great original manual for martial arts instruction. *If the warrior's heart turns bitter or dry, the fight will be lost.* But even the great martial art teachers, Drona and Bhishma, go down in action. Drona gets tricked by false news of the death of his son (who happens to have the same name as a dead elephant); thereafter his head is cut off. And Bhishma, confronted by a woman warrior, refuses to fight, is pierced by a thousand arrows, and lies like a porcupine for the next fifty days, giving his dying and sacred wisdom, such as women are the root of all evil but also righteousness and pleasure. You have to admit, there are some other great bloody moments: Jayadratha causing the death of Arjuna's son, and, in retaliation and with the help of a solar eclipse, Arjuna severing Jayadratha's head with one bold arrow and sending it like a cannonball into the lap of his meditating father. This is an example of how a curse can return to its owner. Then there is Bhima, who crushes his cousin Duhsasana with his great mace, ripping open the man's chest and drinking his blood and then comparing it to mother's milk, all this in revenge for Duhsasana having dragged wife Draupadi by the hair and attempting to strip her sari from her lovely body. This is, you say, tantamount to rape. Then Draupadi, who since this shameful incident fourteen years ago hasn't tied up her hair, washes her dark tresses in the same blood.

Finally there is Krishna: blue incarnation of Vishnu and chariot driver for the great archer Arjuna. Like the *Iliad*'s narrative pause to describe the great panoply of civilized life welded into Achilles's shield of war, similarly, the *Mahabharata* interjects a moment of great hesitation: Arjuna, on the cusp of battle, falters. For eighteen chapters and seven hundred verses, Arjuna slumps back in his chariot and has a crisis of conscience. *If I start this battle, I will have to kill my brothers.* Why indeed do we fight?

This is, after all, the *Bhagavad Gita.* Even though Mohandas K. Gandhi admitted in his autobiography that he was introduced to the *Gita* by his British Theosophist and Transcendentalist friends, as he becomes the *Mahatma,* he confirms the book's wisdom. Krishna urges Arjuna into action—there is individual duty to one's talents and purpose in life, and, it should also be pointed out, to one's class or caste in life. Arjuna was born to act, to be the archer and to fight. Actions are tied to actors for reasons that are beyond our knowing. One man's calling may be another man's sin, but he cannot impose bad will or karma on himself if he acts without desire, passion, or self-concern. He must kill with detachment. This is his duty to God, for it is God who wields justice. Action is his path to freedom. Victory and defeat are the same. Birth and death are illusion.

Whew. But wait. A foolish personal thought: did it matter that Asako, *cool as a cucumber* after months of indecision, put on John's ring and took the plunge? Does it matter that that is why I am even here writing this? It's hard to theorize away my birth, especially since I rather enjoy being here. Years later in Hiroshima around 1972, I'd have tea and pecan pie with Mary MacMillan. The pecan pie was very special, made with difficulty in Japan, a place with no ovens and no molasses and no Kentucky bourbon, although I doubt any bourbon was in the pie. The pecans had been sent to Mary Mac from her home on the Louisiana delta. She'd come from a long way away to leave the Jim Crow South. During the war she'd taught high school at Topaz, and then she left for Hiroshima and served the Methodist mission there for the next thirty-five years, witnessing the aftermath of the atomic bomb and caring for children of the hibakusha. She expressed to me her great respect and love for John and confessed rather matter-of-factly that she always wanted to marry him. She drawled like the southerner she was, *Oh of course he met your wonderful mother Asako, and I was so happy for them. And, well, here you are.* Now that I think about this, I wondered what Mary Mac had been thinking in the day, about a common mission to God's purposes, about making John happy because certainly such a man deserved happiness, or perhaps it was due to Mary Mac's romantic interest. I was too young to ask such stuff. Mary Mac had taken instead a monastic path, matching her actions to her ideals.

Mary Mac accompanied me on the requisite tour of Hiroshima, to the Atomic Dome, to Sadako Sasaki's bronze statue laced in chains of paper cranes, and finally to the old Peace Memorial Museum. At the door of the museum, Mary Mac said, *I have been in there many times, and you must see it for yourself, perhaps by yourself. I will wait here for you outside.*

Inside those dark rooms was hell's terror made real. A city and its people rendered to an expanse of black ash. Charred and melted flesh, clothing turned instantly to shreds, cloth patterns welded onto skin. Masses of disfigured, naked dying people moving ghostly toward water, collapsing, floating in black rivers. Metal artifacts—tricycles and lunch pails—transformed into twisted, corroded rubbish. Stopped watches and empty silhouettes of human forms cast onto concrete, the living originals turned to vapor.

Mary Mac waited for me at the door. I walked out into the sunny humidity of a haunted Hiroshima. We did not speak. There was nothing to say. By chance or perhaps inevitably, life chooses you.

Two years previous, I had seen a play at the Los Angeles Mark Taper Forum entitled *In the Matter of J. Robert Oppenheimer.* I have a vague memory of a chain-smoking genius who confronts the demons of his great scientific intelligence and talents and that singular accomplishment of the Manhattan Project at Los Alamos. What is frequently written about Oppenheimer was his interest in Sanskrit and translation of the *Bhagavad Gita.* It is said that the Trinity test in the Jornada del Muerto desert was named not after the Christian trinity of God the Father, the Son, and the Holy Spirit, but after the Hindu trinity: Brahma, Vishnu, and Shiva—Creator, Preserver, Destroyer—and that as that first iconic mushroom cloud burst into Earth's atmosphere, these passages awoke in Oppenheimer's mind: *If the radiance of a thousand suns were to burst into the sky, that would be like the splendor of the Mighty One . . . I am become Death, the shatterer of worlds.*

Vyasa, if you stop a battle for seven hundred verses, maybe the reader should take note. Why can't peace intervene? Why is it that we are eager to get on with the action? Why are we headed inevitably for disaster? Why can't we hold the imagination of violence as a story in our minds so that we can live the value of its lessons in peace and reconciliation? But these are not Arjuna's questions to Krishna; they are mine to the storyteller. I do not know the answers, only that both, the great leader of ahimsa and the scientist builder of the atomic bomb, read and used these seven hundred verses to find solace and meaning for their actions.

You have said that for the Hindu the world begins with sound. Thus it is possible that poetry creates and re-creates the world as the ripple of a single pebble thrown into water, the beat of a drum, a bell chime. But you have also said that all art is political, made in *polis* or community. Poetry is not innocent but has consequences. Twenty-five centuries later, there it is, still rattling around.

In the postwar years in Oakland, until he left with Asako for Los Angeles, John's passing comments in his letters show that he had hoped to get an appointment with Howard Thurman and his multiracial interdenominational project at the Fellowship for All People's Church in San Francisco. There remains no formal paperwork or correspondence about his application, and the Japanese Methodist Conference—a segregated unit within the larger Methodist Church—may not have been willing to part with John's services. From time to time John preached or attended services at the Fellowship Church, and Howard Thurman continued to be a friend and mentor. On January 30, 1948, Mahatma Gandhi was killed; on the following Sunday morning, February 1, Howard Thurman offered from the Fellowship pulpit his memory of meeting and conversing with Gandhi in 1936. John took notes which he then typed into a narrative to be passed on to Alma Gloeckler and others.

Thurman recounted meeting with Gandhi at daybreak for exactly three and a half hours, under a large bungalow tent in Bardoli, Gujarat, following four hours' travel from Bombay:

Never in my life have I been a part of that kind of examination: persistent, pragmatic questions about American Negroes, about the course of slavery, and how we had survived it . . . voting rights, lynching, discrimination, public school education, the churches, and how they functioned. His questions covered the entire sweep of our experience in American society . . . One of the things that puzzled him was why the slaves did not become Moslems. "Because," said he, "the Moslem religion is the only

religion in the world in which no lines are drawn from within the religious
fellowship ... This is not true in Christianity, it isn't true in Buddhism or
Hinduism. If you had become Moslem, then even though you were a slave,
in the faith you would be equal to your master."

As their conversation closed, Sue Thurman asked if Gandhi would come
to America *as the guest of Afro-Americans,* to which he answered that he
would first have to win the struggle in India before he could make other
helpful contributions. However, Howard writes: *Before we left he said that*
with a clear perception it could be through the Afro-American that the unadul-
terated message of nonviolence would be delivered to all men everywhere.

When I met Alma Gloeckler, as I said, who was around the age of one
hundred years, she had a particular gift she wanted me to have. It was a
black-and-white photograph of a group of people taken on a hillside garden
somewhere in Oakland. The photographer had almost chopped the heads
from the frame, privileging the foreground's ivy draping over volcanic
rock, but somehow, what Alma called *our group* is all there. Their inscribed
names have begun to fade from the back of the photo, the script confound-
ing exact spelling:

> *Gerry Cambridge*
> *Alma Gloeckler with Baby Judy Utsumi*
> *Kay Yamashita*
>   *behind is Petrofae Cambridge*
> *Daisy Froderburg Funderley*
> *Rev John Yamashita*
> *Wayne Amerson*
> *Bernice Cofer*
> *Mary Ann Utsumi*
> *Bill Utsumi*
> *Laura Kennedy Robbin*
> *E. J. Kashiwase*
> *Miye Kashiwase*

Alma repeated that this was *our group. Every weekend we would meet and*
discuss things and make a plan. And then we would go, for example, to a restau-
rant that hadn't been behaving very nicely, and we would all sit down and order
our meal.

I nodded without understanding, but Alma was patient and insistent. *Oh, those were difficult times. You have no idea. People didn't want to see the Japanese back. They were very mean and hostile. We had to do something.*

So you all went as a group.

Yes, we were all mixed up, so they had to serve us.

You did a sit-in?

Yes! she exclaimed with enthusiasm. *We did direct action!*

She pressed the photograph into my hands along with a VHS documentary tape about the life of Bayard Rustin. *Bayard,* she nodded, *he was one of us.* In 1942, Rustin traveled for the Fellowship of Reconciliation to civilian public-service camps as well as to assembly centers and concentration camps to support the internees and to rally folks out of bitterness toward activism. In a short report dated October 15, 1942, to John Swomley, Rustin wrote: *When I arrived at Manzanar the F.O.R. group had already arranged a car and I set out immediately and toured for six hours ... This was a great experience and I shall turn in a complete report of several pages on conditions in the camp ...* By the end of the war, Rustin himself would be imprisoned as a conscientious objector who refused any civil participation or pacifist support of the war.

I date the photo to around 1947, when Kay would have had a summer visit to Oakland. In April of the same year, Bayard Rustin set out with fifteen fellow travelers on his *Journey of Reconciliation,* an interstate bus ride through the states of Virginia, North Carolina, Tennessee, and Kentucky to test the abolishment of Jim Crow, and sixteen years later, Martin Luther King, Jr. would write from a Birmingham jail.

My folks came home to a divided community of those who had said yes-yes and those who had said no-no and everyone in between. There was an unspoken partition and bitter heartache, still felt to this day, but everyone was in the same boat generally—hated, feared, shamed, still considered the enemy that had been conquered, whose people had killed *our* Americans. John did not bemoan those years of exile but encountered a larger world and meaning that might never again place him particularly in any one place or home. After so much wandering, I am directed to this unanchored but planetary place of his heart. And Alma wanted me to know something about what it takes to live a hundred years: survival, as you will say, is about the connections between us. For a brief and forgotten moment in 1947, reconciliation met in the contrapuntal. The names are inscribed but the people forgotten, the photograph fading evidence, and the story but a ripple in time.

Dear Vyasa:

I am fascinated by how Homer, Ishi, and you "read," as thinkers and teachers. There is something to say about this, but I cannot quite figure it out now. There is your personal scholarship, the odd encounter with a text that is supposedly written to address this scholarship but, as I now see and admit, misses the mark; but then, there is anyway your humility and generosity in response; well, the teacher in all of you. And there is, finally, my incapacity to really know your thinking, to know the thinking of any reader.

At first, you invoke Ganesha, the scribe dipping his tusk into ink, and you advise that *Om Ganesha* precedes any undertaking to remove obstacles. Thus, in your usual way, you gift an open path, and I am grateful.

On to your namesake, Vyasa, which you say means *to sever and then to join or construct,* and this is true about the work of the poet who deconstructs events and remounts, re-members them to understand. In the storytelling of the *Mahabharata,* Bhishma vows celibacy in order not to have progeny who will be condemned to kill each other. However, the poet-narrator Vyasa, despite this prophecy and perhaps desiring a story, intervenes with his aging member to comply anyway, fathering two sons, and thus must tell the story of what transpires. You think about this, about Vyasa who is implicated in this great epic about civil war, and that neither narrator nor scholar may hide from the responsibility of their personal relationship to history or to ideas. You have said that in the Vedic tradition all histories begin with the word *itihasa;* thus it is said, and you understand this to mean that every history is a story told, weighted by the knowledge of the teller. It is, you add, this responsibility, not only accountability, that offers truth to storytelling. Knowing that the *Bhagavad Gita* is itself a later intervention, reinterpretation, and extension of verses added to the *Mahabharata,* you feel that my family stories are also welcome. Well, if you say so.

Love,

Mary MacMillan 1942

LETTERS TO
Death

Dear Ananda:

We met at a dinner party where, you would say, all things can be resolved as long as, you would also insist, someone takes the time to arrange the flowers, polish the glass, set the stage. Well, it was in fact my dinner party, created in the havoc between classes and the usual short notice, so I doubt there were any flowers, though tea candles to create atmosphere and give a hint of reflective sparkle to obscure the untidy, unpolished household, but most certainly, some sort of stage was set. The dishes, platters, glassware, table, and cloth napkins all belonged to my parents, participating in a past generation of dinner parties, a backdrop of simple elegance to create a sense of celebrative belonging passed forward into time with John's ever-present prescription, that the conversation be *scintillating*. John loved to cook *bold and fearless*, which meant that he never test-tasted anything while cooking; he wanted to experience the same surprise as his guests. And he expected a good return for his kitchen labors: that those who came to the table provided their own surprises, new thoughts, fellowship, and laughter. Whether we are aware of it or not, every dinner party recalls another and another, the glasses filled, raised, and emptied, different reflections, new lips, a tradition to honor the savoring tongue, the savoring spirit. You understood and made me remember the conditions of this tradition, remembered to me also your aunt and her dinner parties in Paris, your lost childhood in Cambodia, and the dear friends who have feted you along the way in Southeast Asia, London, New York, Philadelphia, Salt Lake City, Seattle, Long Beach, Sacramento, San Jose, and Berkeley. I hear your laughter across many tables, blessed with irony, beauty tips, and your basic rule that homosexuality resides as a hidden gift, even if in minute degrees, in every man, woman, and child. This is the empathy your presence implants in each of us, and it is the reason you are both my brother and my sister.

Mao Zedong famously said, *a revolution is not a dinner party*. And to that he added: *writing an essay, or painting a picture, or doing embroidery.* But now, you will say, we should have learned in the very least that the *insurrection* and *act of violence by which one class overthrows another* may obliterate not only the conditions of inequality but everything that gives pleasure to the ideals of living in equality and brotherhood. This obliteration of pleasure is the smallest portion of the violent horrors we have come to know of such revolutions. It is no small feat of spirit that out of the ashes of genocide, you in your body and intellect have chosen to know and to remember the ancient past in order to reconstruct, recuperate, and to nourish, to push aside old pain to recapture lost elegance, dignity of spirit, and the luxury to speak with wit and frankness. You might argue that the essay, the painting, and embroidery may be in themselves small but significant revolutions. Here, then, I cordially invite you once again to a place at the table, to my dinner party, and I humbly ask that you arrange the flowers.

Art in the Garage

Today is August 6. On the same date in 1945, Enola Gay ejected Little Boy into the city of Hiroshima to birth the atomic age. And two days later, Bockscar dumped Fat Man into Nagasaki, a city rich in a history of controlled encounters with hairy, unbathed redheaded barbarians in pantaloons—nanbanjin—and vestiges of their architecture, cultural curiosities, west folded into east, churches and temples, all vanquished with equal vengeance. This is the learned memory the August summer recalls; exiled, wanderer, prodigal, dead, all return home, under the grace of a broad, slippery moon shedding cool relief in the heated night, to grieve, to be reconciled, to be released.

For as long as I can remember, and in every garage that he occupied in a series of three houses in Los Angeles, John had a carpenter's worktable with a power saw and tools. And above the table, there always hung a framed oil painting of the Oakland West Tenth Methodist Church. We never thought to question the presence of this painting that always hung next to handsaws, hammers, and fishing rods in the structure that served as shop, gardening shed, and car port. We simply expected to see it there as if to greet us as we arrived from church, a picnic, a summer camping trip. The painting never entered the house; it was a part of John's particular handyman's workspace, always there to watch over him sawing and refashioning the headboards of a bed into a shelf, polishing and prepping his reels or golf clubs, a transistor radio tuned to the voice of Vin Scully and the Dodgers.

In L.A., the first house we lived in was a typical Southern California bungalow on Fifth Avenue near Jefferson, a several-block strip of Japanese American businesses—groceries with tofu and fresh fish, butchers, dry cleaning, pharmacy, curios, dry goods, sweet shop, dentistry, and optics—which reopened in the postwar 1950s to service the returning Japanese community, young nisei families hoping to jumpstart their lives with kids and the old American dream. John's next ministerial appointment, the Centenary Methodist Church on Jefferson and Normandie, was at the very center of this community, at least for me. Our neighbors on one side were an elderly retired white couple named the Thydens, and on the other were two African American families living in a stucco duplex. Cookie Green and I could open our bedroom windows and talk across the narrow corridor lined with calla lilies between our two houses. At one end of Cookie's house, her mother, tall and elegant, practiced her vocal scales and songs. I imagined her to be a famous opera singer, but more possibly she was the soloist in her church choir. And at the other, Mr. Green seemed to have the television tuned perpetually to the commotion of cowboy and Indian epics. During the school year, my sister and I walked a block to Sixth Avenue Elementary, and during the summers, we pranced in and out of a small geyser of cool water spouting from a single hose over the sloping front lawn.

This house was raised over a half basement you entered through slanted shed-like double doors outside the back porch. John used this slender space under the house as a storage area. I have an unclear memory of watching water slip over the concrete patio and under those doors. Perhaps it was my fault, enjoying the curiosity of spraying water steaming over hot cement, filling our plastic wading pool, then discarding the flowing hose. Or perhaps it was a broken pipe or a particularly rainy season. Whatever happened, the basement flooded, destroying the stuff stored there. So many years later, Asako dampened my enthusiasm for this archive of letters. *Oh, you are missing Nobu's letters to John from Italy. They were destroyed in that basement flood at Fifth Ave.* I imagine a cache of letters bound in string, script on thin paper, aerograms perhaps and postcards, European stamps and postal marks, Nobu's confident scrawl and the return address: *N. Kajiwara, 100th Infantry Battalion, u.s. Army,* all turned to pulpy mush.

In his written memory of Nobuo Kajiwara, John never mentioned the lost letters. Instead he remembered:

It was in the summer of 1943 when I was in summer session at Garrett that Nobu completed his basic training at Camp Shelby in Louisiana. He dropped in to see me at the Garrett campus in his going overseas furlough in full uniform. I didn't know how we were to spend his few days, but since he liked good jazz music we decided to go to Chicago's southside . . . just west of the University of Chicago . . . We found our negro night club and walked in to see all black faces. When they saw me a Japanese and another in full uniform, they gave us the best seats in the place as cherished ethnic buddies. We were treated royally—we dined and drank and had our fill of Chicago jazz. I returned to spend the rest of that summer in Ethnic and Theological studies, and Nobu left to take the military transport bound for Salerno Italy.

This Chicago visit is recorded in photographs of John and Nobu in front of the Buckingham fountain. On July 11, the following summer, Nobu was killed at the Allied front, somewhere north of Rome.

Perhaps also lost to wet pulp were the letters from a second childhood neighbor and *lifetime friend,* Tyler Eitaro Nakayama, who, as a pharmacist, joined the 442nd medical corps. Of Tyler, John wrote:

> *He served in Italy, France and Germany, and when the war was over he discarded his past life and entered the College of Arts and Crafts ... In the course of the years he changed his name ... to Willard Tyler, the nickname his boyhood buddies gave him ... He is the one who had sent me many European gifts and to this day I treasure an Italian brass mug ... I still have his old jazz wax records of Bix Beiderbecke and others. I cannot break them up to discard them.*

John does not speculate about why Tyler abandoned his former profession or his Japanese name or even why Tyler disappeared so completely from a lifetime of friendship. One friend died; another survived. Both disappeared forever.

So it was Tyler who left John with the oil painting of the West Tenth Church. Flipping through a box, I found a signed pencil drawing, a tableau in a stone house with a medic bandaging the arm of a man, his wife and two children surrounding him, the image of a saint or Mary mounted in a relic box on the wall. Posted in the doorway just outside is a soldier with a rifle. In lieu of letters, Tyler drew for John this moment of war somewhere in Italy. There are also two watercolors and another pencil drawing, unsigned, but likely also Tyler's work.

Among John's old collection of 78 shellac jazz records there are three albums: *A Duke Ellington Panorama, Meade "Lux" Lewis Blues Boogie Woogie,* and volume two of the *History of Jazz: The Golden Era.* There are also scattered collections with Bing Crosby and others, but no Bix Beiderbecke. Knowing John, he met someone along the way who showed an interest and gave Bix up to another enthusiast, someone who likely walked away with my title favorites: "Sentimental Baby" and "There Ain't No Sweet Man Worth the Salt of My Tears."

Sometime in the 1960s, the West Tenth Methodist Church was demolished to make room for the Acorn public-housing project and a freeway through West Oakland, to this day a disastrous urban plan of displacement and enforced segregation. This was about the same time that we moved to our second L.A. house, another parsonage, in the Crenshaw district. In 1964, as predicted by his history of hypertension, John suffered a massive stroke and the paralysis of his right side. He struggled through physical therapy to regain his ability to walk, to write, and to speak, but he would never be the same. Yet, the following year, on the hottest summer day in August 1965, he must have stood with us, leaning unsteadily on his cane, out on our Virginia Road sidewalk listening to fire engines roar across the city, smoke billowing far to the east in Watts. The riots were distant but near enough to our old house on Fifth Avenue and to the Centenary Church. What John thought, I do not know, but he stood there disabled and impotent to act or even to speak. I was too young to understand the sad impossibility of John's dream of racial integration; though in a few years I would join the volatility that was the tinder for riots—*power and by any means necessary.* Japanese and African American urban communities had been bound to each other by labor migration, racial prejudice, and housing covenants. Two decades after the war's end, the promises of racial democracy and economic well-being did not pan out for everyone.

For my family, this was the summer when everything changed. Eventually John took disability retirement from the church, and Asako taught elementary school children for the Los Angeles Unified School District, beginning a teaching career of nineteen years and replacing John as breadwinner. From this moment on, I understood John to be always dying, believing that I might look away and he would be gone. Though at times an anxious feeling, it was just a new reality, and besides, he always wore that smile. My sister and I grew up boomers, our cultural nutrition a mix of soul and rock, Aretha and Baez, *I Spy* and *Captain Kangaroo.* We became part of a sansei generation who would seek to recover the history of our people's incarceration, protest the racist war in Vietnam, join voices and ideologies with militant paths to power and revolution.

Meanwhile, an old collection of jazz wax records gathered dust near a newer turntable, no longer equipped to play at 78 rpm, and Tyler's painting of a demolished church and disappearing neighborhood still hung faithfully over another worktable, greeting always our arrivals and departures.

Mada
ikiteru yo

Ananda, you have invited me to walk in meditation with you, but when we do walk, we chatter and laugh endlessly about everything, foolish nonsense, and yet with the pleasure of the deepest sense of our living moments together; we live a noisy meditation. I suppose we would not have it any other way. To be honest, the silent meditation we experience is when we are apart, distant in our own worlds, writers in separate universes. That is perhaps the state of the writer and the letter writer, a meditative state graced by the imagination of the presence of the other. Ah, but you would say that meditation is wordless, the breathing space in the hollow of the mind that whispers through and between and beyond. There is no such thing as noisy meditation or musing meditation or even prayer meditation. It is complete attention to a bodiless timeless everywhere, a wholly mindful space between life and death. Of this, I believe I am incapable. But push me out into warm waters to swim, become a fish, better yet, a jellyfish, a transparent billowing community, pulsing through liquid, slipping into and under muffled and cyanese silence. Maybe. As a child, nightly I witnessed the severed heads of unknown people swirling around my dark bed; terrified, I slipped into water and swam away.

By contrast, Tomi landed in the desert of central Utah. Nothing but sand and sage. At the end of 1942, Tomi turned sixty. She had immigrated to Oakland through the Port of San Francisco at the turn of the twentieth century at the fair age of eighteen, married Kishiro Yamashita, and bore seven children, one every three years from 1903 on. John speculated that he and his siblings were exactly three years apart because Tomi breast-fed each of them until age three. I never heard this from anyone else in the family, but maybe John had a good memory; plus this was the sort of raised-eyebrow detail John liked to tell in the middle of some dinner party. Between raising kids and breastfeeding, Tomi also worked as a seamstress in Kishiro's Yokohama Tailors shop. In 1932, when Kishiro died, Tomi opened the Mayfair Cleaners, taking in laundry and sewing jobs. When people talked about the issei generation, you got the message that these were the real pioneers who labored, who broke their backs, scrimped and saved, lost their shirts, suffered the confusion of language and cruel humiliation of hatred. Then at the end of years of continuous labor, the final indignity was incarceration. As my mother Asako would say, *no rest for the wicked.* Not to say that I've had any sort of comparable life, but I'm around the same age as Tomi was when she walked into Topaz. She lived to be a few months short of ninety, so let's say she was about two-thirds

there. Knowing Tomi, she probably wore a corset all through camp; nothing would stop her from looking svelte, with proper posture and bosom in
place, a woman of vitality. When Tomi was at the end of her life, nearing *wicked rest,* John flew to Chicago to be her hospice nurse. She opened
her eyes one morning to find John cleaning up her room and grunted with
some irritation, *Mada ikiteru yo.* When I think about Tomi, it's this phrase I
remember: *You know, I'm still alive.*

In Tomi's photo album, there were a few of those rare photographs
taken in camp: a larger group picture arranged before a tarpaper barrack
and a smaller photo of Tomi and four women set against barbed wire and
the dirt landscape. With some research, I discover that these folks represent the artists in camp sometime around 1944. Of the artists incarcerated
at Topaz, perhaps the most well known were Miné Okubo and Chiura
Obata. Both were friends of the Yamashitas from their Berkeley days. In
the prewar, Okubo studied art at Cal with a couple years in Paris, and
painted frescos with Diego Rivera for the Works Projects Administration.
The Obata family lived in Berkeley, Chiura teaching art at Cal. At war's end,
Okubo gathered her sketches of evacuation to Tanforan and imprisonment
in Topaz and published *Citizen 13660,* a pictorial indictment of those years.
It was Chiura Obata who founded and opened an art school in camp, involv-
ing sixteen artists and eight hundred students over the years. One of those
students was Tomi.

A story I did not know was that Chiura Obata, despite his idealistic
decision to stay in Topaz to create an art school, attempting to bring some
beauty and hope to that ugly episode, was attacked and beaten as if a *traitor*
by a camp fellow. After his hospitalization, the Obatas left Topaz for Saint
Louis, and thereafter, colleague artist and friend Matsusaburo Hibi and
his wife Hisako continued the direction of the art school until the camp's
closure in 1945. It is this later contingent of artists and students, sans
Obata, who pose in that group photo before the Topaz barracks. And in
the smaller photo, Tomi stands among her lady artist friends, Hisako Hibi
and her daughter Ibuki crouched in the dirt. The gifted artist Hisako
Hibi would also have been Tomi's teacher.

At war's end, the Obata family returned to Berkeley, and Chiura became
a professor of art at Cal. Tomi also relocated to Berkeley, and she continued
to be a faithful student of Obata, probably almost until her death in 1972.
Her sumi-e paintings were saved in large rolls of rice paper that John and
I unrolled and perused after her death, spreading them across the tables

and floors. What we discovered were repeated attempts at the same scene, but there was always at least one of each that was, well, perfect, and this I assume to have been Obata's example that Tomi tediously tried over and over to reproduce. John chose the most perfectly rendered and had them framed, and told guests that they were Tomi's work. They were unsigned, so who knows? Tomi would have been one of Obata's oldest students, if not the oldest, his senior by three years. After so many years of dogged persistence, Obata granted Tomi some sort of official status as a deshi with a name and hanko. John said, *Oh it was honorary. She was never very good. Obata must have thrown in the towel.* But what were those unsigned paintings that hung all over the house? Some sort of fiction, I suppose.

Rolled up in the center of a heavy pillar of Tomi's artworks was a canvas painting, which for some reason had been stored and forgotten. An oil painting, a still life of yellow flowers with black centers, squash and fruit in the foreground. The painting is signed *Hisako Hibi, Topaz 1945* with an inscription in the back of the canvas: *Milky Weeds and Sunflowers.* Matsusaburo Hibi died only two years after the war in 1947, but Hisako returned to San Francisco and lived a long and productive creative life. The painting was perhaps a parting gift, removed quickly from its wood frame, sent away to wander far from the sadness of camp, to remember friendship.

What, I ask you, is the true value of art? In Tomi's precariously kept collection of paintings, there are also original Obatas and this Hibi still life. I will have to pay an expert to refurbish and remount the Hibi. The Obatas are variously dotted with brown spots, evidence of the paper's acid slowly returning the work to dust. This is even true of the carefully framed unsigned work, assuming it is Obata's. Everything is slowly fading. Although sold to sustain their lives, neither Obata nor Hibi would have necessarily assigned great monetary value to the product of their art. Not that I don't feel guilty that this art isn't better preserved, but like the letters, it's a bit of clutter and bother. Don't museums make choices? What to hoard; what not to hoard? But, you may protest, Obata and Hibi would find this dilemma crass. The subjects of their art demonstrate their aesthetics and ethics. Art is a tool and a process. In a time of war and intense hatred, Obata and Hibi sought escape and resistance. Exiled to the desert, Obata sought the meditative solace of nature. Within the confines of barbed wire, Hibi sought the ordinary in daily life. A mindful resistance mediated between life and death.

As for Tomi, John always said that camp gave his mother a break from constant labor, that being able to spend her days painting was a hidden gift. Leisure in confinement. A cruel truth. How many other of Obata's and Hibi's students also came to enjoy for the first time that sense of creative pleasure? Were they not laborers removed from the backbreaking work of harvesting fruits and vegetables, the tedium of slicing and canning fish, washing and cleaning the houses of the rich? Obata, Hibi, and even Tomi had pretensions to another life, and Obata was beaten up by someone who resented that presumption and the arrogance of the mind's freedom, or perhaps what was perceived to be the blind innocence of intellectuals and aesthetes who did not recognize their basic condition as fodder to exchange for the lives of American POWs. In war, nothing is fair. In the nationalist agenda, you are either for or against. Tomi refused to the end of her life to become naturalized as an American citizen, her stubborn protest of the indignity of incarceration. No questionnaire could define her loyalty. She had sacrificed her youth to raise and educate two children in Japan and five others in America.

Years later, I've separated only those few drawings that Tomi signed and to which she put her red stamp. In fact, there is only one scene on which she imprinted her hanko, that of Yosemite Falls. You can take a look and judge for yourself. Let's say it isn't the technique but the spirit of the work, in the spirit of her teacher. Slipped in among those same rolls of paintings on rice paper was the shiny 1960 *Life* magazine cover featuring Grandma Moses on her hundredth birthday. In 1960, Tomi was seventy-eight, camping out with us in Yosemite, hiking to the falls and Half Dome. Undoubtedly, she and I, then a nine-year-old kid, walked together in noisy meditation.

Granma, what does your name Tomi mean?

Means rich. Tomi rich.

What about my name Tei?

Means happy. Means you are very happy girl.

Studying in Japan years later, I look up the word *tei* and find the meaning: chastity. I also discover that my American name has basically the same meaning. She was right. I am *very happy girl.*

I bet she was still wearing her corset.

アートスクール

1943

Oct. 18th, 1966
17508 So. Catalina Ave.
Gardens, Calif. 90247

Dr. Thurman,

Your letter to me in May was a breath of fresh
and was a high point in a changing summer. It
so kind of you. And when my sister Kay brought
e books from you, it was more than encouragemen
ited to write you a meaningful letter in answer
use I know you might understand my groping afte:
's ideal. Again, after my stroke in January of
when I lost half of my mobility and speech, I've
trying to ascertain the extent of loss of mind
idgment and memory. Happily I don't feel much
here and the change of activity is a Godsend.

I thought _____ your books, but was elat
and the "Temptations of Jesus" and the "Medita-
s of the Heart". I shall pass on my own copies
he others. I am sure too aware of all thot
experiences we are trying to relate where I am.
abeth Yates' biography was very revealing and tl
me up to date on your activities and readings.
all cherish Lawrence's story of "Viewing
he Coast of Africa". I thank you so much.

As you may know, at Garrett at Evanston durin
var when I was endeavoring to finish my seminary
les, the only relevant or should I say most rele
word I heard in Christian studies, was the
ion week meditations you came to Evanston to gi
s stimulated by Professors Nels Ferre, Paul
ar and the writings of Reinhold Niebuhr but the
e experience was most disappointing. They thot
s neurotic (coming from a War concentration Cam
hot quite articulate how they had no patience t
en. This handicap I shall always carry. In
stian studies, I had much kinship and broadenin
orizons in the apocalyptic and eschatological
ings of Christianity. So to this day I appreci
his area in Jesus' perspective (as you say in
and Death vista of eternal life). Especially,
this posture or understanding, anxieties even

119

Under the
Healing
Wings of
Suffering

Ananda, you have referred me to Buddha's sacred biography of multiple rebirths in the *Jataka Tales*. If there are 547 tales, one assumes that Siddhartha Gautama's journey to enlightenment took 547 cycles of life folding into death folding into life. In one tale, he is the wealthy and altruistic prince Vessantara who, from the moment of his birth, gives alms to the poor and likely all his toys and other princely possessions. But finally he gives away a magical white elephant that brings rain to the kingdom, and losing rain is too much. What about the public good? So he's sent into exile. In preparation for this, he gives away seven hundred slaves, seven hundred chariots, seven hundred this and that. You wonder if he had seven hundred pairs of shoes or seven hundred bracelets, but no doubt there were seven hundred bling. Then he leaves with his wife and two children on a chariot with four horses. Along the way, he gives away the horses and chariot, and the family makes the arduous trip across rivers, through forests, and up mountains on foot, fed and protected by the kindness of people, devas, animals, and trees. Now there's a bad guy, a Brahmin, Jujaka, who knows Vessantara's inability to refuse a request. Of course, the tale never says this inability is a weakness or an obsession or a personal rule that can't be broken or that Jujaka is a foil to test Vessantara. The journey to enlightenment is a stubborn path of faith. Plus, there must be some reason here to stick it to the faithless Brahmins. In any case, taking advantage of this opportunity, Jujaka asks for the prince's two children, whom Vessantara finally gives away. Then, the god Sakka, disguised as another Brahmin, comes around and asks for the wife as well, so she's also sent packing. The good news is that the kids are sold to the old king, the grandfather; a subsequently wealthy Jujaka dies from overeating; and Sakka removes his disguise to return the wife to her husband. Since the wife is a gift, Vessantara can't refuse. You have to wonder how she was his to give away in the first place, but this is the fourth century BCE. The old king goes into the forest to retrieve his exiled son, but the exclamation of their reunion is too much, and they all collapse—one supposes, in blissful death. But there's a happy ending: a red rain falls and revives the family; the white elephant is returned; seven kinds of gems fall from the heavens so that Vessantara can store them and always have gifts to give away; and Jujaka goes to hell.

As a story, the happy-ending denouement seems unnecessary since a blissful reunion should be its own reward, and it seems excessive to return to Vessantara his seven hundred slaves and seven hundred chariots, magical elephant, and a storehouse of gems so that he can be charitable to his heart's content. A story about a rich prince divesting himself of everything including his children and wife had to be a story not only for the greedy Brahmin and the rich, but also for the ordinary and the poor. A poor man could divest himself of three things that might be everything, and that would be enough. And a happy ending could soften the additional step that's actually required beyond generosity of things: the relinquishing of desire. Even if his children and wife were not his to give away, Vessantara's willingness to leave behind his emotional and sensuous desire represents a higher ideal. All this leads, you remind me, to an ascetic existence, disengaging the body from the spirit, disencumbering the preoccupation of self from wisdom. It reminds me of Gandhi's autobiography, a story that reads like a contemporary Vessantara, as he makes a series of sacred vows to give up everything: animal flesh, sex, cooked food, milk, clothing, medicine, and formal education for his children. The body is a vessel for action and must be primed with physical truth; no kind of abomination can enter a body prepared to enact or receive truth. Ahimsa and satyagraha cannot be attained except via a stubborn and rigid control of the body. And Gandhi reminds you that the thing you are giving up has to become disagreeable to you in order for this to work. It goes without saying that this is not a recipe for every body.

By 1936, when he'd pared down his living to a pair of sandals, a homespun cotton wrap, a pocket watch, and his glasses, Mahatma Gandhi met Howard and Sue Thurman under a tent in Bardoli, Gujarat. At the end of their meeting, Gandhi asked if the Thurmans would sing a particular gospel song: "Were You There When They Crucified My Lord?" Howard wrote that Gandhi explained his feeling that the song expressed *the root of the experience of the entire human race under the spread of the healing wings of suffering.* I confess my antipathy for the image of the crucifixion, my agnosticism regarding the resurrection, and my instant feeling of strangeness about Gandhi's request of his African American visitors. You remind me that Gandhi's spiritual foundations were profoundly Jainist, thus nonviolent, fasting, celibate, and that his very physical presence—the shrunken, half-naked, baldheaded brown man that has become our iconic memory— was itself a spiritual and political statement. Then you point to another twentieth-century representation of the sacrificial body, that of the burning monk Thich Quang Duc, self-immolating at a Saigon crossroad in 1963. Now then, it's possible to imagine the Thurmans and Gandhi, their three voices singing that gospel song under a tent in Gujarat, and the resonance of its meaning. Years later I find Paul Robeson in John's record collection, and I hear Robeson's voice. An old recording, his deep bass baritone blessing the depth of the song's sorrow—there, I find myself present under the hovering shadow of those *healing wings of suffering.*

Vyasa traces the root meaning of memory: to be mindful, to care for something. Thus memory is practical, creating and re-creating, re-membering, the process by which anything is cared for. Memory is passed on so that we may continue to care. But what about unwanted memory, the traumatic and violent memory of horrific and terrible deeds, of genocide, torture, imprisonment, irrevocable loss? Gently you remind me that to suffer is the human condition, and attachment is its cause. Trauma means to hold on to anger. Memory and loss must be cared for in order to lose anger.

In the mid-1940s Howard Thurman published two essays, "Deep River" and "The Negro Spiritual Speaks of Life and Death." Decades previous in 1903, W. E. B. Du Bois also published a book of essays, *The Souls of Black Folk.* Both the mystic theologian and the materialist social historian recuperated the *sorrow songs* as the ineffable force of a collective memory, captured subversively, minded fiercely and tenderly, and cultivated despite the assumed erasure of history, identity, culture, and family. To both scholars, searching for artifacts that have traveled over time and generations, these songs bore witness to suffering and are psalms that continue to resonate the persistent promise that a social and political future can be forged. *Were you there? Tremble. Tremble.*

Howard Thurman died in 1981. Three years later, John died as well. I don't have a memory of ever meeting Thurman but knew of him through John and also Kay, who hosted *Dr. Thurman* on his visits to Chicago. Having visited Boston University to view Thurman's collected papers, I know the correspondence, books, letterpress meditations, and recordings saved by Kay and John are but a miniscule archive, the significance of which is small but very personal. It was Kay who, after many years, brought the two men back together via correspondence, but it was not a fluid correspondence. John's file of saved copies show that he may have never sent what he drafted, that he felt tentative before the task, wanting to be honest but also to impress his friend and mentor. Thurman, for his part, scribbled notes of encouragement:

> *I keep your letter of October 1966 always in my desk. At least twice a*
> *month I read it for sheer joy and keen delight. Please please my friend*
> *will you write—You have so much to say and your thinking runs so deep*

transcending much of Western & Eastern provincialism. Why not get a
manuscript ready let me honor yourself by writing a foreword. Also let me
send it to Harpers my publishers.

The event of John's massive stroke in 1964 forced him into retirement, finally blessed with time to read and to think but without the physical and mental energy to fully accomplish the complex articulation required of that intellectual exercise. I knew that because of John's disability, we as a family were given his complete presence as full-time father and house husband, but I also recognized that we had lost the possibility of knowing his original and capacious intellect, his sharp wit and finely tuned social sensitivity. John's post-stroke writings indicate that he thought perhaps that the stroke had filtered away the unnecessary, as if wisdom could be held in the perfection of a haiku—a poetic excuse that I'm willing to embrace, except that I'm a prose writer who likes to carefully connect the dots before I erase them. I mourn the loss of John's mind because the man who remained for me was prodigious, the space of my growing years filled by his generous and contagious spirit. This archive of letters and papers recovers something, but it is filled with gaps and John's procrastination; that is to say that, when his mind was truly alert, he had no real time to write, and he did so at the last moment and without the concerted care and editing that writing requires. Perhaps Howard Thurman knew something I have not discovered, and this trust must have given John energy. On the occasion of Thurman's seventy-fifth birthday, John joined others to write articles in his honor for the festschrift *Common Ground.* John's odd title is "The Creative Stature of Genus Homo Sapiens." I hesitate to critique the article. I've read it over and over, and I still don't know if you need to assume the premises of belief in a *Creator* first, or if the argument requires the careful assistance of a meticulous and knowledgeable editor. To me it is classic John, consisting of the stuff of his preoccupations and exhibiting the influence of Thurman's personal and revelatory mysticism while reconciling the philosophical repercussions of Darwin, Freud, and Einstein with contemporary world politics, the Cold War, the civil rights movement, and the inequities of global resources. His key words: *life abundant, elation, joy and laughter, verve and vitality, the creative dimension of man.* John is heavy-handed with the use of the word *man* to mean all human beings, but in those days, I guess we were all men. Whatever the end product of his only published writing, I have to smile that I lived in a home where someone held forth over dinner to say in so many words: *We are finite creatures with minds to wonder and explore imaginatively and infinitely . . . If we can discover the way to steer society to serve the best and creative interests of man, we will rightly liberate him . . . If we are freed from basic poverty, we must be able to grow in an atmosphere that nurtures beauty, harmony, and peace—essential for free and full growth . . . One's soul has to live forever untrammeled and unshackled to any fixed era or culture, if it is to be free and fluid in that era.* Perhaps it is beyond editing; it is a meditation framed between life and death.

One day in New York City, I took the #1 to 125th to meet Olive Thurman Wong. She greeted me from her open apartment window and tossed the key down to the street. She'd prepared a table of tuna fish salad and banana bread, and we toasted our meeting with ginger ale. She had recently retired as a librarian specializing in costume studies. She was an accomplished designer and theater director. I don't know what Olive thought, but there's a kind of understanding that passes between preachers' kids. I think what may have been true for both Olive and me is that our fathers were very busy if not consumed by their calling and the needs of others, their time and concerns beyond their immediate families, and that suddenly we grew up and were a curious and rebellious exception and unexpected challenge. I also think that our presence humanized and made practical the practice of their ideals, but in the bother of it all, I wonder if they did not consider Vessantara's divestiture or Gandhi's asceticism. From the point of view of the kids, whatever our messy fates with an imagined Jujaka, I think Olive and I came out okay. The one thing I can say about Howard and John is that, whether they fully approved or not, they were each the foundation for our independence.

I want to show you something, Olive said. She pointed to a Japanese doll on her kitchen shelf. *Your father gave that doll to my sister Ann and me.* Then she recalled her happiness in moving to San Francisco in the summer of 1944, when she scuttled the plan to leave early for college in order to remain in the Bay Area as her parents founded the Fellowship Church on Octavia and Post. The family lived on the top floor, and the church functioned below. Down Post Street lived a communal group of activist Quakers and con-scientious objectors who supported the church's work. This group called themselves the *Sakais,* after the previous owners of the house they occu-pied. Among the Sakais were Kay's friends and colleagues, some work-ing for Nisei Student Relocation, in particular a young man named Caleb Foote. And just across the street from the Sakais was a boarded-up grocery and fish market under an old Victorian house where Asako and all her eight siblings had been born. The center of the old Japantown, vacated by one community and housing another. Olive recalled that they had decorated the walls in the church with Japanese art while through the window you could see the racist images of war propaganda on posters and billboards. Olive sighed, and I contemplated our intersecting paths. *I studied Daoism,* she said. *I think it's true that everything is integrated.* For dessert she served baklava, and as we licked the honey from our fingers our conversation wandered, and Olive had a thought. Lillian Smith. Had I read this author, her novel, *Strange Fruit?*

In the same year that the Thurmans moved into Japantown, Lillian Smith published *Strange Fruit,* a novel about an interracial couple in a small town in Georgia. The U.S. Postal Service and even some booksellers banned the book for lewdness, though it still became a best seller. Five years later Smith published a book of essays, *Killers of the Dream,* which can be understood as the critical underpinning of her fiction; an analysis and critique of white supremacy, sexual repression, racism, and the church's split personality of high moralism and Jim Crow segregation. Also significant about Smith—though perhaps never mentioned at the time—was that she was a lesbian, and her novel is dedicated to her partner, Paula Snelling.

Lillian Smith's novel acknowledges the connection of the title *Strange Fruit* to a poem and song written by Lewis Allan in 1937 and performed by Billie Holiday in 1939 at Café Society in Greenwich Village.

Southern trees bear a strange fruit,
blood on the leaves and blood at the root,
black bodies swinging in the southern breeze,
strange fruit hanging from the poplar trees.

"Under the healing wings of suffering" . . . "strange fruit hanging from the poplar trees." *Were you there? Were we there?* Memory cared for.

Ananda, I have a last bone to pick. In the cycle of life, what is justice? Are we to understand that the karma of one's deeds, good or bad, will eventually catch up—if not in this life, then in another? There is some satisfaction in the possibility, for example that white people will become colored, or the rich will know poverty, but I don't suppose that's the greater spiritual plan. What about those who suffer now? Are they living in the skin of their other because that is life's lesson? If they knew and believed this, what would they do? But what of those victims of unspeakable atrocity, holocaust, slavery, genocide, terror, those slaughtered in the path of war or nature's blind violence? *Holocaust, slavery, genocide*—these are only words, only words. It is beyond all comprehension. Howard and John studied and struggled all their lives to understand, to extricate the truth to create a path for others, for Olive and for me. In this regard, you will say that I've been a miserable student.

Howard Thurman in his day was criticized for *turning mystic,* which to those at the political front seemed to be a turning away from active participation and leadership. Again and again he writes about Jesus as a social activist and rebel, about the relationship of mysticism to social change. If you witness suffering, what is your responsibility, your duty? Sue Thurman asked Gandhi this very question. His answer was, in essence: you must embrace love and, without fear, actively not cooperate. This was perhaps also Thurman's answer—his mysticism therefore was not a disengagement with social and political life. No social movement could move without the healthy confidence and integrity of each individual, requiring the full engagement with a life self-empowered to act without personal desire or fear, to act with complete generosity.

In the 316th Jataka tale, a monkey, an otter, a jackal, and a rabbit prepare together to observe charity under the full moon. An old Brahmin sitting by a campfire begs for food. The monkey gathers mangoes from the trees. The otter collects fish from the river. The jackal steals a roasting lizard and a pot of curds. But the rabbit, able only to offer grass, throws itself into the fire to be roasted. The fire is cold to the rabbit's dear gift, and once again, the god Sakka abandons his old Brahmin disguise and, with lilting strokes of his brush, paints the memory of the rabbit onto the face of the moon. A wisp of smoke reminds you of the burning fire.

THE GARRETT TOWER

Garrett Biblical Institute, Evanston, Illinois

AUGUST, 1943
VOL. XVIII, NO. 4

*Religion in a Time of Crisis

Howard Thurman

CURIOUS indeed is the fact that at a time of crisis men must be constantly reminded that the crisis does not mark the end of all things. It is of the nature of crisis so to dominate the horizon of men's thoughts that everything that is not directly related to the crisis situation seems irrelevant and without significance. At such times men seem to accept the contradictions of experience as being in themselves ultimate. The crisis throws everything out of proportion, out of balance and the balance seems always superficially to be on the side of disaster, on the side of negation. At such moments right is seen as being "on the scaffold" and wrong as being "on the throne"—the human spirit is apt to cry all men have bowed their knees "to Baal and I, I only am left." If the contradictions of experience are ultimate, then the conflict between right and wrong, good and evil, order and chaos can never be resolved and human life is caught eternally in the agonizing grip of a grim and eternal struggle between these two forces. But such a dualism has never been able to satisfy the deepest searchings of the mind and the heart of man. The human spirit at long last is not willing to accept the contradiction of life as being ultimate. There continues ever a margin on the side of the good—yes, the ultimate destiny of man is good—this affirmation becomes the ground of opti-

DEAN HOWARD THURMAN

*The editor is glad to publish the text of the Commencement address delivered by Dean Thurman at Garrett on June the seventh.

mism and inspiration in the bitterest crisis when the times are "out of joint," when men have lost their reason and sitting in their "sepulchers of gloom watch their dreams go silently to dust." It is the peculiar task of the preacher to recognize this deep urge within man and to call it to bear witness at all times, but particularly at such a moment as is our own, now that the whole round world is rolling in darkness.

If the ultimate destiny of man is good then he must find *in the present* a way of life that is worth living—he must maintain a faith that can be honestly and intelligently held—he must work for the kind of world in which even the weakest may find refuge and refreshment—in which the smoking flax will not be quenched; nor the bruised reed crushed.

A Way of Life That Is Worth Living

We are all of us in quest of a way of life that is worth living. We want to feel that we are engaged in a total enterprise that is meaningful. There must be a sense of something at stake in the day's experience. If this is not true for us then life grows dingy on our sleeve and days are but days and nights are but treacherous interludes before the monotonous round begins anew. It is for this reason that war, despite its terror, wreckage and stark tragedy, makes so great an appeal to men, women and even children. It is not because there is no

5-5-67

Dear John—

I keep your letter of Oct, 1966
always on my desk. At least twice a
month I read it for sheer joy and
keen delight.

Please, please my friend will
you write — You have so much to
say and your thirty runs so deep
transcending much of Western + Eastern
provincialism. When you get a manuscript
ready let me know yourself by writing a
friend. also let me send it to
Harpers my publishers.

I had a good though short visit
with Kay while going through Chicago. She
told me that you were flying a trip
to the Far East. I had hoped to get
down for a visit before that bus

Dear Ananda:

To seat Thurman beside Gandhi beside the Jataka tales is a kind of fusion accomplished by the fiction writer. I'm not trying to say anything new, simply speculating, perhaps attempting to extend Homer's thoughts of poverty and forgiveness and Vyasa's insistence on contrapuntal reconciliation.

I want to answer your query regarding the dinner party, which again I admit is a facile ploy to begin our conversations. And yet the dinner party is where my memory of John resides, in his love of cooking and gathering and his insistence on *scintillating* conversation. What troubles you is the invocation of Mao's quote regarding revolution and my response that violent revolution may destroy, well, the dinner party. This, you say, is true, but to say it in the context of genocide and holocaust is completely incommensurable. I agree. What I wanted to suggest are your own gifts that grace the idea of the dinner party—graciousness, art, and ceremony, love of beauty, that reanimate life that can never be the same.

This incommensurability further troubles you as I have placed disparate historic traumas—Cambodian genocide, African slavery, Japanese American incarceration—together, and they are not the same. Obviously, they are not the same. You wish me to *tease* them apart, but that work has already been done. Numerous and immense volumes of historic recording to name the historic conditions, the crimes, the victims and the perpetrators. Where does such cruelty come from? Are we not all complicit? There are no commensurate traumas, but if we do not draw parallels, how may we be empathetic? How may we together be held responsible? Together show compassion? How may we be friends in times of duress?

You speculate on Gandhi's vision of *the entire human race under the healing wings of suffering,* and you say that for the Buddhist, suffering is the human condition and attachment is the cause of suffering. Again, in drawing together the disparate, I have collapsed the images of crucifixion, lynching, and self-immolation seeming to generalize the paths from suffering to spiritual enlightenment, to make universal that which is not. And again, I have no intention of making everything the same, but rather in the spirit of Vyasa's contrapuntal to arrange close encounters. These encounters cause you to wonder at the body's capacity and sometimes desire for pain and sacrifice and the parallel paths to divinity and humanity, art and cruelty.

When speaking about the artists in camp, in particular Obata and Hibi, you wonder if I've not romanticized their practice in suggesting that their art avoids reality or seeks escape through nature or the daily. You think about art and music and poetry performed in other circumstances of incarceration, in death and labor camps, and point out that such creativity, using tools and any scarce materials available, is *an impulse to sustain one's humanity* and is an act of resistance. And perhaps we should add an act of witness. You remind me that while art may be spiritual practice, it is also political.

Finally, you refer to this writing as memoir, perhaps family memoir. I don't know why I felt surprise to see your reference to *memoir* or why I resist the idea, although I have thought of it as memory. You may wonder at the obvious, but I have had no formed definition for this project except an intuition that you would listen and be attentive and somehow understand.

In peace,

LETTERS TO
Laughter

Dear Qohelet:

You're a preacher's kid. When we met, we recognized each other immediately, that PK je ne sais quoi, like we're supposed to be doing something significant eventually or actually, like we were raised with everyone looking on politely resentful, assuming we knew, when we didn't, and thus, perpetual strangers in a world of blessed woe, primed by difference to serve. One day I heard you lecture, and I turned to you after and marveled, *You gave a sermon.* You answered, *All my lectures are sermons.* I thought, maybe mine too. Frustrated PKS. But you must have been really frustrated because finally you entered the seminary and got a master of divinity. I could never do this. Well, you believe, which is kind of necessary. One day I came home from junior high school and announced at dinner that I'd discovered a philosopher named Jean-Paul Sartre and a great idea called *existentialism.* I can't remember what John said, but that was the beginning. I have been that kind of PK, heading out in another direction which turns out anyway to be the same. I figure you will understand, that you'll know the skinny and funny of it.

Recently I saw again yet another staging of Shakespeare's *King Lear,* and I wondered about those good and bad daughters, silent tribute versus false fawning and the misreading of love and honor. Do daughters naturally aspire to be Cordelia, or is this an impossible and romantic notion upset by character and circumstance? *No, no, no, no!* cries Lear to Cordelia, broken and unwilling to further challenge his fate. *Come,* he encourages her, *let's away to prison.* And then these his last words to his daughter:

We two alone will sing like birds i' th' cage.
When thou dost ask me blessing, I'll kneel down
And ask of thee forgiveness. So we'll live,
And pray, and sing, and tell old tales, and laugh
At gilded butterflies, and hear poor rogues
Talk of court news, and we'll talk with them too—
Who loses and who wins, who's in, who's out—
And take upon 's the mystery of things
As if we were God's spies. And we'll wear out
In a walled prison packs and sects of great ones
That ebb and flow by the moon.

I am drawn to memories in which we *live, and pray, and sing, and tell old tales, and laugh*. Ah, but to *laugh at gilded butterflies*, this must be the satiric laughter that I am prone to, but John would say that this is not truly laughter, not the laughter that preoccupied his thinking. It is not laughter *at* but laughter *within*, I think, that concerned him. I am growing old searching for this kind of laughter, and where is he now that this laughter is needed most? Meanwhile I have found myself beholden to the lost possibility that we *take upon us the mystery of things as if we were God's spies*. Perhaps this has been the meaning of these letters, though surely no mystery is revealed here. Simply, we have been together for a time to try.

CLEAR
CLOUDY
RAIN
SNOW

Waffle Iron & Vacuum Cleaner

Wednesday, August 26, 1942, Kiyo, housed with her one-year-old baby in a converted Tanforan racetrack horse stall—Barrack 20, room 18, wrote in her diary:

> *Today is our second anniversary, and a very disappointing one at that. I should learn by now, judging from my past two birthdays, not to look forward to any special day, for the disappointment is too great, and the hurt too deep.*

Not only the fact of the evacuation but marriage itself—that is, in terms of celebrative memory—seems to have been generally a bummer; but then, guys just seem to forget. Once you get married, even if it's the most glamorous wedding of the year, it's not about you anymore; it's about them. This has got to be a sore point in many a marriage, but here further compounded by exchanging a house on Parker Street in Berkeley for a one-room horse stall. Four months previous, Kiyo stood in the rain for several hours with her baby in front of the First Congregational Church in Berkeley, waiting with the rest of the Yamashitas, and every other Japanese American in Alameda County, to board buses en route to a "relocation center." The day before, she and Sus had been emptying the house of furniture into the early morning hours, packing up their belongings, then sleeping briefly on a mattress on the floor, waking to frantically pack the rest.

To make matters more intense (notice I don't say *worse,* but it's got to be worse), the entire Yamashita family crowded into the small Parker Street house in those final days to make sure they would *evacuate* together. Sus was the first son and thus head of family, but this was *his* family; that is, Kiyo's in-laws. What a crew. There was mother-in-law Tomi, brothers-in-law John and Tom, sisters-in-law Kay and Iyo, sister-in-law Chiz and her husband Ed and six-year-old Kiku and, finally, an adopted son, Tom Misumi—twelve altogether. It must have been mild chaos. From Kiyo's sparse and concisely penned diary, we know she packed a crib and mattress and formula for her baby—justifiable and practical, considering. But from stories told, we know that for some reason the Yamashitas also packed an electric waffle iron and a vacuum cleaner. When I read the official edict *to bring only what you can carry,* the waffle iron and vacuum cleaner seem like items in a tall tale. I don't know how the group of twelve got all their stuff and a heavy vacuum cleaner from the Parker Street house, about a mile away, to the Congregational Church on Channing near the Berkeley campus, but I remember my father reminiscing about that vacuum cleaner, parked on the sidewalk with the rest of the luggage. Maybe it was a Hoover upright. The old ads say, *Give her a Hoover and you give her the Best.* Maybe they pooled their resources and gave Tomi the Hoover for *her* birthday. Kiyo was right to be upset; what woman wants a vacuum for her birthday? They were likely told that the vacuum had to be left behind, but knowing John, he may have surreptitiously tagged it, then slung it on with the luggage, hiding it under the tarp, as the truck pulled away in the rain.

I cannot find in any correspondence or documented memory any mention of the vacuum cleaner, but Kiyo makes two brief mentions of waffles in her diary, on June 4 and August 26 of 1942. The June 4 entry says that they *all went to the ironing room and had a feast of scrambled eggs and ham and waffles.* Ironing room? I think I know why the ironing room. When John told his story, he said, that of course they were the only family with these electric appliances, but when they plugged them in, they blew the fuses and shut off the lights. When this happened, he'd yell out in innocent protest through the porous wood slats, *Hey, what happened? Who did that? Not again! Someone, turn on the lights!* As if no one smelled the waffles. So with that consequence in mind, the waffle *iron* would require the requisite power supply found in the *iron*ing room. *Meet me in the ironing room, honey. You can iron while I waffle iron.*

The second mention of waffles is on August 26, the unfortunate *second wedding anniversary.* It's a concessionary entry toward the end of Kiyo's day. *Chizu planned a waffle party for our anniversary, and we all enjoyed waffles. Nobu Kajiwara made the party possible by bringing the eggs and butter, and he and Ish and Hachi were there besides the rest of us.* Maybe Chizu, and for that matter Nobu and John, knew Sus's ineptness at celebrating, and surely felt Kiyo's disappointment and difficulties caring for a baby in scarce circumstances. Or maybe any excuse for a party was necessary to subvert hopelessness. I think about that smuggled-in waffle iron and the preciously saved eggs and rationed pats of butter, and I feel that defiant strain of rebellion and extravagance that for better or worse marks the family. But then, there is Kiyo's final sentence on this day: *Sus went to play bridge at the Nishimuras and did not return until very late.* Ah well, they tried.

I wonder about the waffle iron and the vacuum cleaner, if they made it from Tanforan to Topaz, from California to Utah. You always read about Topaz and the dust storms that lifted the desert sand in blinding swirls and penetrated everything, seeped into the barracks and frosted the interiors in thick layers. You can't imagine that the Hoover upright survived such abuse. This wasn't urban household dust or even an occasional button or bug. This was grit and living creatures—scorpions—that might have ground the gears, dried up the lubricating grease, torn the bag, snuffed out the motor. Or maybe not; maybe the Hoover Company distributed their machines around Topaz to test *the Best*. Daily, Topazians swept the outside from the inside back outside. Bringing a vacuum cleaner to the Utah desert was like the surreal project of the Walrus speculating with the Carpenter, who *wept like anything to see such quantities of sand,* and wondering *if seven maids with seven mops swept it for half a year . . . that they could get it clear?* What had John thought as he shoved it onto the truck. Maybe, *What the heck, maybe it will come in useful.* Or maybe Tomi really wanted to keep it and doggedly insisted, so *urusai,* and hauled it over, and besides, *They didn't confiscate it, and who's defining what we can carry anyway?* And then later, John's amusement over the absurdity of its bulky useless presence. Good for vacuuming horseshit. The first stories I heard him tell about camp were these, chuckling in glee, as if to assure me of comic relief.

I wonder why, after packing up for storage an entire household, these two items remained unpacked. Okay, I know: someone insisted on vacuuming the empty house before finally vacating it. This idea in the face of forced evacuation seems to me so Japanese-hyphenated-American—the tacit recommendation to leave your previously occupied space cleaner than you found it. How many picnic and campsites have we left cleaner than we found them? How many rentals? Dorm rooms? Borrowed kitchens? Concentration camps?

And okay, how about waffles for a last breakfast before heading away to an uncertain future? What John would call a *sayonara breakfast.* Get some sustenance in the belly before being exiled to prison camp. I recall that one of John's favorite and most famous meals was Sunday brunch, which he believed must consist of corned beef and hash brown potatoes, eggs, sausages, bacon, and waffles with liberal amounts of butter and syrup. Waffles were special, celebratory, and I never understood why until now.

Somewhere in the Topaz desert: bits of gears and electronics, a rusty molded iron plaque in square patterns, the flat double prongs of an untethered electric plug. Somewhere in the dust and scrub this extravagance, this spontaneity, this comic relief.

Slow

When the sub,

somehow it does not se

The average person only

privileges.   It seems t

far as his own interest

all his citizenship dut

goes to the polls and v

of the average citizen.

The "question"

a more significant role

today?"

We are living

the central theme of ou

undergoing radical chan

Germany|, Hitler's progr

people, in fact it has s

strife and disorder have

government.   In Italy,

Russia| is toiling under

In the last fe

rapidly lost ground in t

on trial today."   The ve

back until today, the Un

stronghold of democracy.

seen indications of disc

in the midst of plenty,

in misery.   And they are

good or bad.   With the i

deplorable conditions ex

f citizenship is first mentioned to us,
suggest anything very meaningful.
ks about it in connection with voting
of importance to him only in so
concerned. Ordinarily, he considers
d responsibilities discharged when he
That I believe , is the usual attitude

e to ask this everyone is. "Have we
tizenship to play, in our country

world of change. Indeed, change is
lives. Governments everywhere are
nd nations are facing crises. In
endangering the liberal ideas of the
d democracy. In Austria, internal
ght about a definite anti-democratic
inni is exercising a rigid dictatorship
eign of communism.
rs representative governments have
vor of dictatorships. "Democracy is
ontiers of democracy have been pusshed
States seems to present the last
ever, even in these United States are
t and despair. People virtually starvin
ons of people out of employment are
ing to risk a change of any sort whether
ration of the "New Deal" to relieve the
s in this country, we see a definite

Sometime around 1910, Tomi boarded the Chiyo-Maru to chaperone eleven young women, all picture brides, from Yokohama to San Francisco. We date the trip to around 1910 because Chizu, who seems to be one or two years at the time and you figure, according to John's calculations, still breastfeeding, is in the photographs. The tallest and most strikingly beautiful young woman in the group must be the future Mrs. Suzuki. The story was that Tomi worried the entire trip about arriving in San Francisco and the eventual meeting with her picture husband, who was shorter and not, in Tomi's opinion, much of a matching beau. If Tomi was five feet, who knows what tall was in the day, but Mrs. Suzuki embraced her fate, and the rest is history.

The Suzukis' two sons, Goro and Michio (nicknamed Mike), grew up in Oakland around the West Tenth Church with the Yamashitas. The fathers were both tailors, colleagues in the business who both also died early in the prewar years, Mr. Suzuki in 1929 and Kishiro Yamashita in 1931. At the time of his father's death, Goro would have been twelve. Growing up in a closed community, you imagine that the Suzuki boys got absorbed from time to time into the Yamashita family. In those years, Kay, who was the family cook for the core seven or eight who then still lived together, remembered that you never knew who or how many hungry buddies John would also bring home for dinner. She would see them come through the door and throw more breadcrumbs into the meat loaf. John called this Kay's *Depression meat loaf,* a loaf of veggies and bread with a hint of ground beef.

John, five years Goro's senior, remembered coaching him for a speech contest. I assume John tweaked, directed the speech's emphasis, and Goro, age seventeen at the time, won the contest, the 1934 gold medal from the Japanese American Citizens League for "Why I Am Proud to Be an American." Not to take anything away from Goro's personal vision, but in John's papers, you can read at least three versions of the speech with John's editorial changes and oratorical instructions for cadence, emphasis, and significant pause. John recommends and pencils above the lines in red: *slow & pondering each word, casually, solemnly, meaningful, stylishly slow, weighty, feeling, taper off, rise, strong & full, come down softer, pause, whisper.* He then underlines words for emphasis: *crisis of democracy, citizenship, selfishness, idealism, sacrifice, humanity.* You can see John orchestrating Goro's oratory with a fine baton. With this speech, they—Japanese Americans—would save America for democracy. They would needle into the hearts of those JACL judges, get them on to their patriotic feet to cheer, and, as they say, not a dry eye in the house. Well, it was the middle of the Depression, and they had no idea what would happen seven years later. Actually, knowing myself a high school teenager under John's tutelage, I have to bet he mostly wrote the speech, titled in John's versions: "The Significance of Citizenship in a Changing World." And after, John suggested matter-of-factly, Goro, a shy kid, got the chutzpah to be a performer. This is one of those beginnings that, I guess, could have gone either way: preacher or comedian.

Maybe John's providential intervention is a fiction and its own chutzpah since Goro was also known to croon like both Bing Crosby and Paul Robeson. Twelve years after nabbing the JACL medal, Goro got hauled off to camp like everyone else. *Oh yeah,* says Asako, *here we were arriving in camp, and there's Goro Suzuki greeting us with a band and singing "Ol' Man River." It was really absurd.* Apparently over the years, Robeson changed the lyrics, but only those who were there in camp know what version Goro sang, whether the upbeat jazz of Crosby or the spiritual force of Robeson. Maybe it was a mix to meet the irony of the situation.

What does he care if the world's got troubles?
What does he care if the land ain't free?
Colored folks work while the white folks play . . .
Getting no rest till the judgment day.
I keep laughing instead of crying.
I must keep fighting until I'm dying.
And Ol' Man River, he just keeps rolling along

Eventually, Goro Suzuki refashioned himself for the stage and television as Jack Soo, the nickname *Su* assuming a Chinese surname since anyway all Asians look the same; it wasn't really a lie. It was more like a serious joke. In those days there was no way to get out of camp to go on the road with a Japanese stage name. Juxtaposed in these stories of Goro/Jack is heartfelt idealism with oppressive racism, and somewhere between impossibility and indignity, the funny and absurd arises. I sense here a wry comedic thread of irony, the sort of mismatch of picture bride to picture husband, of Crosby to Robeson, of entering camp on the river of the Ol' Man. If Goro, over the years, cultivated the classic nisei deadpan he made famous on *Barney Miller,* as the detective sergeant Nick Yemana (is that a Japanese surname anyway?)—humor honed on adversity—John was the guy whose eyes lighted up. Years later John would take me to see the Roger and Hammerstein's musical *Flower Drum Song.* And there I saw Jack Soo (Goro) crooning and tap dancing with Pat Suzuki. *Hey,* John chortled with amusement, *I grew up with that guy. I gave him his first big break.*

Sometime in 1978, I remember finally meeting Jack Soo at the Centenary Methodist summer church bazaar in Los Angeles. I say I met Jack Soo, since his famous comedic and performer's face was by then so familiar, but the man I really met was Goro Suzuki, who, ailing from cancer, stood with John among the booths of snow cones, teriyaki sticks, and flipping ping-pongs into bowls of goldfish. On a hot August weekend, John stepped forward unsteadily on his cane. The two men had perhaps only seen each other a few times since the war years. One of the last encounters may have been as long ago as 1949 in Oakland when John presided over Mrs. Suzuki's funeral. And though John may have wished for an old joke, one last con-summate wisecrack, Goro, unable to speak, held John's hand and wept.

Japanese Bite the Dust

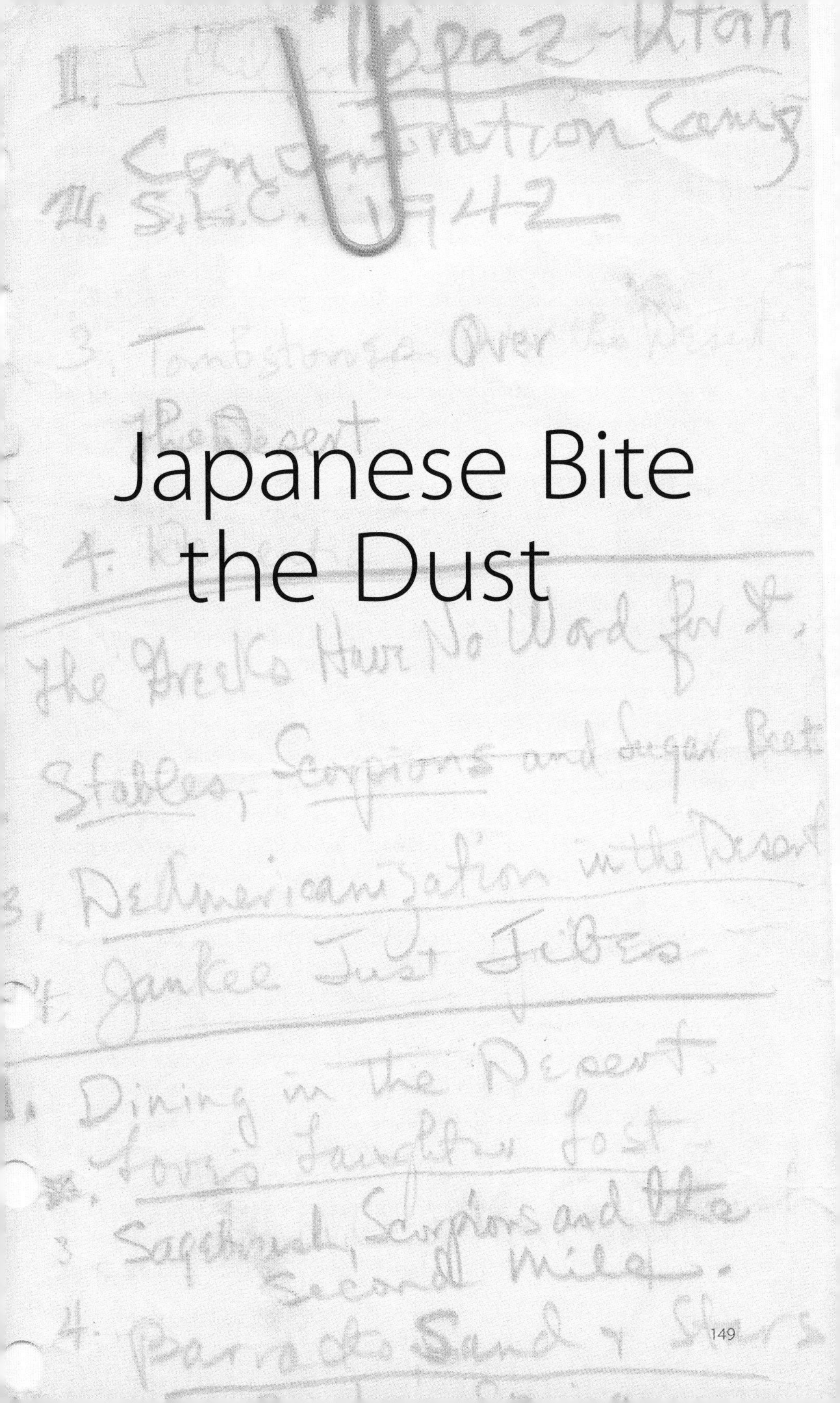

Qohelet, I had expected to write funny stories, but all the laughter here seems contained in another dimension, and I think no one is laughing. Well, there is the problem of context, as in *let's away to prison . . . to laugh*. There is nothing romantic here about laughter. It's not about some expression of indomitable spirit. It's just necessary, a survival tool, but also a way of perceiving. John always expressed a dislike for the *guy with a chip on his shoulder*. He thought if you couldn't get rid of that injurious chip, that it would find its way into your heart and corrupt your being. You could never be a whole person carrying about a wounded sense of being wronged. Your anger would surface and hurt others, usually those who loved you best. He thought camp was the most unjust, cruel, and oppressive event of his life, but he was adamant that it would not control his character, well, he would say, his soul.

Then there was his job, that of being a preacher, a pastor, a minister—all rather loaded words for the job, but nevertheless, the job. I finally opened the dusty boxes marked *sermons* and found dozens of seven-by-ten-inch black spiral notebooks of years of Sunday preaching, but also of weddings and funerals. As required by the church, the names of and dates for each wedded couple and each dead person are carefully noted, along with the particular ceremonial proceedings, prayers, songs, and personalized speechmaking. There were the baptisms as well. Over the years, he must have married, baptized, and buried hundreds of people. Beginnings and ends, cycling forever. I had forgotten this ceremonial part of his job, the required institutional, communal, and spiritual blessings that mark our lives. Plus, there were holidays, and a congregation's illnesses, trials, and tribulations. You could but shouldn't do this job without conviction and sincerity, and not with a chip on your shoulder. All his writing over the years, sermon after sermon, even at the end when thinking became muddled or compressed, expresses his deep and passionate belief. Agnostic that I am, I fashioned an idea about John as tilted toward social justice and the eventual ideas of liberation theology; that too was his job, but the empathy upon which the community depended, as if their daily bread, was based in an expression of what he called love and creative laughter. There is an intangible sense that he embodied, for others, this way of being. Therefore he was wanted there, always, at beginnings and endings.

A Catholic-raised friend of mine has said that the reason for Sunday mass, despite what anyone might believe about the place of religion or, for that matter, Sunday in the week, is to remind us of our better selves. In those war years, whatever the rest of the country on Sundays thought of their better selves, the old Oakland West Tenth Church bunch at Tanforan and later Topaz attempted to gather to reflect on, most likely: *Why us?* John remembered giving an early sermon at Tanforan entitled *Dust, Diarrhea, and Degradation.* He called it the Three Ds. Only the sermon's title remains. I want to know what reflective Bible passage inventively accompanied this sermon, and I have to imagine the significant pause at the sermon's close—did they laugh, grumble, scratch their heads, or weep? And his final words . . . *Now let us pray.*

John's notes show a series of titles for camp sermons, among them *Tombstones Over the Desert; Stables, Scorpions & Sugar Beets; DeAmericanization in the Desert; Dining in the Desert; Sagebrush, Scorpions & the Second Mile; Barracks, Sand & Stars;* and *Blossoms in the Dust/Desert.* I have no idea what *Jankee Just Jibes* refers to, though it could have been a popular jazz tune, and *Greeks Have No Word for It* is pretty cryptic. John does feature two titles on his key theme, laughter: *Love's Laughter Lost* and *For Tomorrow's Laughter.* I wonder if substituting *laughter* for *labour* is significant? A second list must be typed later, and the titles show greater anger: *Incarceration & Bestiality,* though I wonder what he meant by bestiality; *Delinquency in Deprivation; Desert Dementia—Sagebrush & Sanity.* My particular favorite, however, is *Japanese Bite the Dust.* Only the titles exist. Good grief, I think, they could be comedy routines or songs, but they are sermons.

A copy of one sermon given at Topaz on Sunday, September 26, 1942, does exist, and indicates that perhaps the list is at best facetious. John's title for this sermon: *Created in the Image of God.* Here he reflects on his free life at home near the San Francisco Bay and at school at Cal with *100 careers to choose from.* Considering he's a Japanese American talking about the Depression years, it sounds a bit exaggerated, but I suppose he's describing it as a kind of Eden. But then there's the reality now of living literally east of Eden, in *Block 6, barrack 3, Room E. 5 cots in a room . . . And you and I facing a brutal reality today. We can only see DUST—desert barracks and very little of the future. The picture is dismal—it isn't rosy—it is unpredictable . . .* From these casual thoughts, he jumps to observing that they will soon live ten thousand together, and that, in short, there's work to do. Now to the meat of his sermon, Part II, which is to say that man has a brain and, like God, is empowered to create the world around him. He refers here to theologian Reinhold Niebuhr and to the Nobel-winning scientist-physician Alexis Carrel, who turns out to have done eugenics research in Vichy, France. But what did John know, confined within barbed wire? And who among the Topazians knew Niebuhr? John believed in human progress and that science and philosophy and theology were all in cahoots, on the same higher path for the greater good of man. You wonder about the scripture attached to this homily; there is no record, and what could it possibly be? I wonder what those folks suffering dust and degradation thought that September Sunday. Did they get up and walk out into the desert and think: *I have God's brain, and there is work to do with God's brain.* One state catty-cornered to the southeast, in that continuing desert, in a place called Los Alamos, men were hard at work using God's brain.

Qohelet, now that you're a bona fide preacher yourself, you'll say it's easy for me to make fun of these camp sermons. After all, I wasn't there. And the unfairness of hindsight. Someone had to tell these forlorn and humiliated folks that they were remarkable and godlike, that *love's labour* could be lost but not *love's laughter*. Again, I've failed to know laughter. Maybe you'd say laughter is not about happy or sad. Perhaps it's about beginnings and endings and being there.

TOPAZ - UTAH - CONCENTRATION CAMP - 1942

INCARCERATION AND BESTIALITY

DESERT DEMETIA -- SAGEBRUSH AND SANITY

THE DESERT SEES NO EVIL - THE DESERT IS SILENT

DUST FOR THE DURATION

JAPNESE BITE THE DUST

DELINQUENCY IN DEPRIVATION

THE MAN WHO (NEVER) CAME BACK

TOMBSTONES OVER THE DESERT

YESTERDAY"S LAUGHTER AND TOMORROW"S TEARS

dust, barracks and tears

DIARRHEA, DELINQUENCY AND DEATH THE DEVIL

DUST, DIARRHEA AND DEGRADATION

DESERT, DUST AND DIARRHEA

SAGEBRUSH, SCORPIONS AND SANITY

DE-AMERICANIZATION IN THE DESERT

loves laughter lost

THE DESERT IS SILENT

STABLESM SCOPIONS AND SUGAR BEETS

SAGEBRUSH, SCORPIONS AND THE SECOND MILE
DINING IN THE DESERT
BARRACKS , SAND AND STARS
WIND, SAND AND STARS
BLOSSOMS IN THE DESERT - DUST
THE GREEKS HAVE NO WORD FOR IT
JANKEE JUST JIBES
TODAY'S TEARS AND TOMORROW'S LAUGHTER

Once upon a time there was

best doctors of the land to atten

and the king was getting progress

of the court who after consultati

wear the shirt of a happy man. T

told them to spare no the horses

search of the happy man. They tr

icing about and choosing a partic

a happy man. He replied, "Yes, h

about over and the week would fin

was not truly happy" They ques

happy man. They then extended ti

went up into the mountains and fo

asked one who seemed to be partic

must be a happy man -- you look

peace with myself out here I'm aw

I think of them I'm worried, I'm

search far and wide and every man

their hopes of finding the happy

resting at a wayside inn, when sud

iately they sprang up "at the end

the man with laughter

They queried him, "You seem to be

replied I'm quite happy, thank you

price for one of his shirts, and

a shirt to my name!"

The laughter of the human so

thing that money cannot buy -- and

of a person. It is something wh

(1949)
(Fall Q.)

For Everything There Is a Season

who was taken sick and he called in the
B ut one by one they gave up in despair
rse. Finally he turned to the wisemen
him t ere was only one cure — he must
immediately called for his messengers,
d with bags of gold they hurried out in
to the seashore and found the people frol-
... at the moment but his vacation was
ck at his work ... drudgery. So he
e others one by one ... failed to find the
ch to the other end of the kingdom and
people enjoying themselves there. They
t peace enjoying the mountain air, "You
ented?" The man replied, "Yes I'm at
my family and its very good. But when
ly a happy man!" They continued their
troubles and rapidly they were exhausting
ll the kingdom. Evening found them weary
hey heard an uproar of laughter. Immed-
laughter surely must be the happy man".
appy, are you a happy man?" "Yes, he
n they produced their bags of gold the
laughed louder than ever, "I don't have

e to be something the embodiment of some-
hich is/the unique and exclusive possession
not be bartered or given away — it is

155

Qohelet, in the final scene of *King Lear,* yet another stage is strewn with dead bodies: Lear and his entire family, all dead—three daughters, two sons-in-law, along with a trusted counselor and his bastard son, and the jester. Well, the jester was done in in an earlier scene, but, for me, his absence hovers over this bloodbath. You see his humor turn sour and satiric, but his fool's honesty and loyalty are not enough to save him. The death of laughter. Thus Lear veers precariously into dementia; he must become his own fool. So it is that, as your namesake declares, even kings who have achieved great deeds, built great houses, and accumulated great wealth, have *no advantage under the sun . . . O how the wise dies just like the fool! . . . All is vanity and the pursuit of the wind.*

I know you know this narrative, but let me, the fool, be your resuscitated guide through the seasons of men. *Further . . . the race does not belong to the swift, nor the battle to the valiant. So, too, bread does not belong to the wise, nor wealth to the intelligent, nor favor to the clever, for a timely incident befalls them all.* That is, if you have a chip on your shoulder, think again about how the chips have fallen, fairly or unfairly and for no good reason. Why are you angry, and to whom or what can you direct your anger? What revenge will finally assuage your pain? *This is vanity and the pursuit of the wind.* And you are a fool if you think that just men receive justice and that fools, like me, are condemned. Human life is vanity, or to translate it more literally: a breath, a whiff, a puff, vapor—illusory and ephemeral. God's hand is pervasive but inscrutable. You cannot know your destiny. No amount of knowledge can make you truly wise. But, and this is a big but, there is a small compensation: the gift of joy. A small, potent gift of the daily. Hold the hand of the small one. Embrace your companion. Give away your bread and your coat. *When times are good, enjoy; when times are bad, see . . . So I have commended joy because there is nothing better for people under the sun, but to eat, drink and enjoy . . . Go, eat your food in pleasure, and drink your wine with a merry heart.*

They say Ecclesiastes contains instructions from an old sage to youth, but like every other ancient text passed dubiously over centuries, its authorship is contested, and some say it never really belonged in this sacred canon. Who is this narrator whose message is read as contradictory, pessimistic, and skeptical, radical in thought, and far afield from the God of divine covenants and prophetic hope, exceptional interventions, and targeted retributions? This is neither the word of God nor of prophets. It is rather the observation of a wise man. Materialist that I am, I find these recommendations finally sane, outside of special promises to special people and special homelands. No one in this world gets saved. Death is the great equalizer.

Homer would note that the narrator of Ecclesiastes likely lived in Palestine under the governance of the great Persian Empire between the fifth and fourth centuries BCE and that the context of his concerns was the crossroads of commerce, the standardization of coinage, the imposition of taxes, and the economic volatility that made humans unequal. And Vyasa would remind us of the traveling nature of story and meaning, the narrative flashes recalling the Sumerian epic of *Gilgamesh* or perhaps the Assyrian sage Aqihar, his *Proverbs* discovered in the Egyptian Elephantine. Who can know the origins of this text said to be penned by the mercurial narrator, Qohelet? Then, Ishi would comment on the anthropology of the narrative, its grounded humanism, and Ananda on its insistence on the worldly as ephemeral and illusory, the cyclical nature of life. But then, you could suggest what John might say—that Ecclesiastes marks the threshold and particular promise of Jesus, his teachings about charity, and, finally, his resurrection and the death of death. I have to quibble greatly with John and admit that I don't believe in the death of death. Not believing in death as the end and great equalizer is in part why, I think, we continue to kill each other.

From time to time in the postwar years, John was invited to preach at Howard Thurman's Fellowship Church. Sometime in 1949, he gave this sermon: *The Laughter of the Human Soul.* Of all the notes, scribbling, letters, and post-stroke essays, this sermon makes most sense to me. Here, laughter is a sign of and a sense of self-integrity, as he says, *feeling at home in one's world,* with a kinship to others and the self-confidence of direction. It has taken me years to understand this very simple but, I know now, nearly impossible way of being. Now I see that at every turn, this is what he looked for in others, and this is what he hoped for, for himself, for his family, for his children. Death was always a heartbeat away, and life, therefore, not to be taken for granted. And laughter allowed for spontaneity and exuberance and extravagance, giving balance to the tough practice of responsibility, play in the diligence of political action, freedom in intellectual pursuit. Even if *all is vanity and the pursuit of wind,* John thought we should stop occasionally for a belly laugh.

Two weeks ago today, John's fourth great-grandchild was born. Born three weeks early, he was almost immediately carted away to a neonatal unit for observation. A sophisticated cart contraption enclosed his six-pound, velcroed-in mini-person, hooked up all his vital signs to a digital dashboard, pumped oxygen to his little nostrils, fluids to his tiny veins, and lifted and wheeled itself onto an ambulance. All this for transport only three blocks away. It was the NASA capsule of an astronaut. In the brief space of his transport, I watched the new infant, not yet a day old, through the thick, shatterproof plastic window. *Where're you going,* I chuckled. *To the moon?*

His dark eyes suddenly opened for the first time and communicated to me his first thought, *Hey, when did I sign up for this?*

I answered, *Astronaut what your country can do for you.* I laughed at my own joke, but the nurses and paramedic crew, all at least a generation younger than me, kindly smiled and shrugged.

Now when I think about it, every one of John and Asako's grandchildren and great-grandchildren opened their eyes to some possible, but in my mind sardonic, and defining first thought.

Are you my mommy?

Fooled you; I'm a monkey.

Who are you?

Who knew?

Do you love me?

They sent me to the wrong place.

You have no idea.

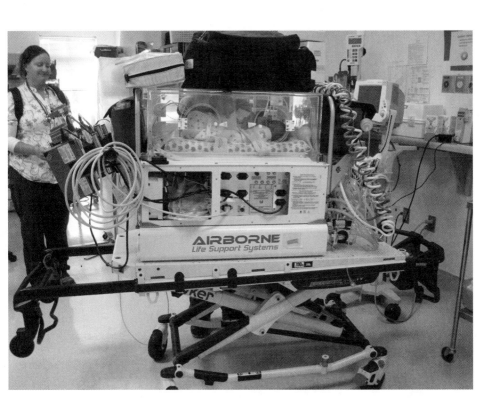

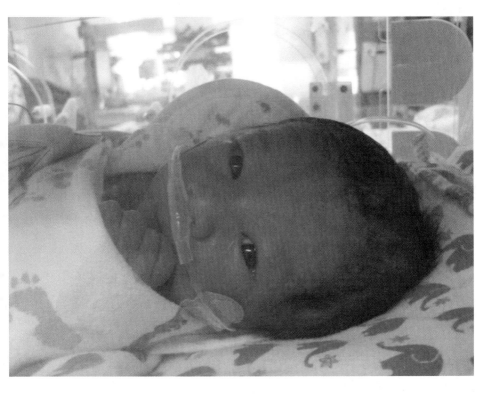

Dear Qohelet:

My first thought is to thank you for remembering the preacher's wife. Never mind the PK, what about the PW? What about her service, so often hidden but assumed? In these moments, you remember the women in your life.

Your poetic sensibility lingers on the waffle iron and the vacuum cleaner as ironic metaphors for camp internment. Amusingly, you wonder what sort of waffle batter, whether a Japanese American recipe, though I assume it must have been some version of Bisquick. In your knowledge of this history, you speculate about laughter as a survival tool but also as a way to reconciliation, that laughter might have invited closure and empathy to the ugly partition of the community into yes-yes and no-no.

You wonder what John thought of Reinhold Niebuhr's view of "Christian realism," especially in relation to the real injustice of camp imprisonment. I suppose I could stop to read Niebuhr myself and thread my speculations into this moment in time, but frankly, I need to stop. My PK devotion has its limits.

As a writer and a PK who read the Bible as partitioned into old and new—a forced narrative of historical continuum—there might be a plot of: this happened and then this happened. But of course, the writer here knows this is absurd; too many narrators. Still, the beauty of Ecclesiastes is that it doesn't seem to belong, that it could be a narrative leap. Maybe I've got it wrong, but this seems to be what sermons tend to do: extract scriptures from their context and leap into contemporary speculations of faith and belief and moral action. What can the past tell the present? Maybe this project has been no more than an exercise in sermonizing, extracting archival letters as if scriptures, to inform or query the present. Only you, a fellow PK, might find me out, my desire for a narrative leap—not a prophetic leap mind you, but just a leap to some kind of clarity or truth.

Lastly, there is your comment that Ecclesiastes is *funny in a very wry way*. I thought about this with some pause, but then it occurs to me that, given the appropriate and familiar contexts and narrative voice, it could all be rewritten as stand-up. It might be the banter of two old men, John playing the fall guy to Jack's dry quips.

All is vanity and pursuit of the wind.
Wind?
Yeah, no matter how you play your cards, eventually poof.
What's the point?
Life is short.
Yeah, tell me about it.
I'm trying to. Believe me, I'm trying.

With laughter to the wind,

Hi   This is an enclosure of actor of Asian Americans
   who   you know who makes a good statement.

How goes the battle?   Yes she liked Capter 5
 Jane and Pat went to Carmel over the 4 day weekend just
over and Asako is getting ready to wind up her career in
teaching in a month. She worked on the yar and I finished
repotting the orchids since Asako went with Seiko to get
100 worth of supplies. I guess she'll take over as orchid
fancier. I'm still on crutches with arthritis of my good
hip and after 3 months guess I'll have to resort to acu
punture. Still drive but got a disabled driver permit.

       So cannot go to 2 weddings or a funeral and have had
to foregoe daily walks around the Lake. What misery!
But it could be worse.
                                      may 27th
       Hey Ma got a ticket for not stopping at a Stop sign
in back of school today and she is mad at hops -- the 1st
in her life!
       HEY HOW ABOUT YOU COLLABORATING WITH ME ON MY
REVISION OF "LAUGHTER AND LIFE"

       YOU SEE I WAS PONDERING ON MY WHOLE LIFETIME THEME
       AND I HAVE BOILED IT DOWN TO (1) Man's finite life but
       his being given an INFINITE SOUL OR MIND
       (2) this accounts for his religious stature or mentality
       (3) this leads to his dreams or eternal HOPE
       (4) his poetry, drama and illusions. and fantasies.

Can you write a child's tale on same -- simple but profound!
Have you any suggestions to develop same.

   We saw the great China Bronze age exhibit
   We saw the Mayan Machu Pichu times of religious lore
   We scouted the Egyptian age --the Cheops age
   We know the Greek pantheon of Gods and the Roman era
   We are well aware of the Judaian story
   You know the Japanese myth and the Indian legend.
   What is the 20th century dream for the moon is barren!

Chiz is getting Kodansha to print my Haiki Images story
about my ten year family history story which we can all
attune to.

   She got a condominium in Rossmoor Homes ou Walnut Creek
way and you Tom has one in Richmond way there which son Bob
is going to stay in and go UC Berkeley. Meantime Ma says
we are set in Catalina Way Gardena and this will be home.

       The Nisei era is ending -- Sansei Ann Dion and Don got
a house in Oakland and Ann is expecting a child in 3 months.
With the passing of Tomotsu -- the Sakai dynasty now passes
to our progeny -- Paul's wife the nurse is a beautiful girl.
Dale the 1sat is getting Bus. Adm. at Stanford and may work
for IBM.

The Gion Shrine in Snow
from the series «Famous Places in Kyoto»
Woodblock print by Ando Hiroshige,
Japanese, 1797–1858
Special Chinese and Japanese Fund
Museum of Fine Arts, Boston

Your farm sounds fine
Say hello to Onofre and wife
We got the picture of Jane II with
Yae and George Kawazoye is celebrating 50th anniversary
on june 20th. Roger Furuno 34 is marrying Wendy on July 5th.

So it goes

LOVE AND PRAYERS

Asako T Dadio

WXC-13202

TO END

Dear Reader:

Asako Yamashita died this year, 2015, at the age of ninety-eight. She would have been ninety-nine on November 10. She was the last, by marriage, of the nisei generation of the Yamashita family. Occasionally I set before her these letters, and she perused them silently without comment. All these years later, the family into which she married still seemed too chatty and too voluble, a garrulous bunch. I think she disapproved of making this correspondence public or revealing private lives to others, and yet they contain a history that profoundly shaped her. Still, aside from honest outbursts, her thoughts remained contained, and she, mostly refusing to say. Living with her for over a decade, I heard her memories surface and recede, change and solidify, cloud and diminish. It is in this way that she bid us good-bye.

With kind and gentle regards,

AND FINALLY

Dear Editor:

You'd think by now this would be over, but there you are waiting beneath every sentence, dipping below the surface of the text, suturing the stuff of it by attachments of word to meaning, sentence to flow, and back to larger meaning. Are you the last critical filter, my best collaborator, or my ideal reader? After your scrutiny, will it be nearly perfect? Done?

How many times have we together read through this thing? Unlike my other five epistolary muses, your concerns have been to make the book in its entirety work. If, for example, I answered their questions about the narrative "I" and "you," you've removed my answers to their queries. Academic questions that offend the literary. Similarly, you've removed my apologies for my lack of knowledge in their fields and also my responses to their technical marginalia, questions about captions and archival access. *Unnecessary,* your marginalia implies and remarks. *Save this for the afterword.* And you've excised digressive references reflecting my fascination for historic serendipity. For example, in 1953, author of the song, "Strange Fruit," Lewis Allan, a.k.a. Abel Meeropol, and his wife, Anne, came to a holiday party at the home of W. E. B. Dubois, where they met and adopted two boys, Michael and Robert, the sons of Julius and Ethel Rosenberg. *Cut; interesting but extraneous.* Phrases, sentences, entire paragraphs have been erased, so many precious words. *This,* you point out, *is the center of the work,* and you proceed to cut the surrounding stuff. Now the meaning can breathe. I think, okay, I'm cool with these cuts. I'm a grown-up writer. I'm breathing.

I think more difficult in this process has been the excising of archival materials. The original draft included entire letters and other associated artifacts. You pointed out that the letters cannot be reproduced in the confines of a printed page at a size that can be read. The handwriting is aesthetically and historically interesting, but who nowadays can read this except my elderly epistolary muses? What remains is a selection of excerpts—of letters, photographs, art, and documents that frame my letter writing as physical gestures to lived history. The reader may access these records for full viewing in the big family archive online. And here is where we insert the link to the archive website: http://yamashitaarchives.ucsc.edu. This is a new literary world, completed by an infinite cyber cloud. It is part of the fictional experiment that I have come to be a part of and to embrace. I mourn the impossibility of print, but you reassure me. This experiment makes possible another way of reading, even as you carefully honor what is written, what I've written here. Your honoring confidence I assume with the vulnerability of an interpreter and translator, matching memory with artifact to the present.

This matching of memory to artifact is perhaps finally the difficulty of what has been attempted here, to speak to the contrapuntal nature of reimagined encounters that are familiar but not similar—that is, metaphorically and fictionally familiar, but not commensurably or accountably the same. You have questioned and argued in some instances for a family story that corrals interpretations around similar histories, and I have pushed in another direction to expand the meaning of living and dead histories and belief systems across bodies familiarly defined by nation and race. Perhaps this was John's project that I have attempted clumsily to complete. We are none of us the same. But there is my family and the familiar you beyond my family, here hopefully resonating.

Well, I owe you a drink. Okay, dinner.

Dinner it is,

YAMASHITA FAMILY TREE

Kishiro Yamashita (12/15/1873–11/16/1931) +
Tomi Murakami (12/2/1882–3/1/1972)

1. **Kimi** (8/8/1902–7/25/1980) +
   Tokiroo Robert Ono (1/14/1888–11/5/1971)

   a. **Theodore Kiyoshi** (6/22/1921–2/26/2015) +
      Barbara Fumiko Yamamoto (10/12/1918–11/25/1998)
      1. **Carole Janice** (12/23/1946–)
      2. **Kathryn Anita** (7/19/1951–)
      3. **Peter Robert** (12/14/1956–)
      4. **Nancy Gale** (9/2/1957–3/10/1958)

   b. **Masako** (b. and d. 1928)

   c. **Martha Chizu** (1/5/1930–) +
      Eugene Shigemi Kiyozumi Uyeki (5/26/1926–9/5/2014)
      1. **Timothy Mitsuo** (8/18/1959–)
      2. **Robert Hideki** (4/18/1961–)

2. **Susumu (Wilfred)** (3/21/1905–9/26/1989) +
   Kiyoko Kitano (10/26/1916–3/20/2005)

   a. **Kimiko Susan** (8/18/1941–)
   b. **Evelynn Haruko** (3/21/1944–)
   c. **Kenneth Akira** (9/11/1945–)
   d. **Michael Shaw** (1/28/1949–)
   e. **Alan Kei** (5/23/1950–)

3. **Chizuru Dorothy** (4/18/1908–4/9/1998) +
   Edwin Kikutaro Kitow (5/28/1899–5/20/1964)
   a. **Edwin Kikuo, Jr.** (8/11/1934–)

4. **Hiroshi John** (2/1/1912–7/23/1984) +
   Asako Sakai (11/10/1916–7/30/2015)
   a. **Karen Tei** (1/8/1951–)
   b. **Jane Tomi** (8/12/1953–)

5. **Iyo (Grace)** (1/23/1915–2/1/2004) +
   Minoru Tamaki (12/23/1918–7/24/2004)
   a. **Ellen Mitsu** (9/11/1946–)
   b. **Ann Yuri** (5/24/1948–)
   c. **Donald K.** (5/26/1951–)

6. **Kiye Kay (Carolyn)** (3/31/1918–5/30/1995)

7. **Isao Thomas** (5/23/1921–12/20/1990) +
   Carol Osaba Shinsato (9/12/1921–5/19/2011)
   a. **John Galen** (11/23/1952–)
   b. **Lynn Robin** (2/14/1956–)
   c. **Robert Charles** (8/15/1957–)

IN THANKS

This project began, for me, with the initial retrieval of a folder of carbon-copied wartime letters from Kay Yamashita to her family. And there were also the photographs and collected artwork of Tomi Yamashita that I've kept over the years since her passing in 1972. Very gradually, as our parents all passed, my cousins also collected letters, diaries, documents, papers, sermons, articles, art, photographs, films, audio recordings, phonographs, and assorted memorabilia. This has been a family project, the bulk of collecting accomplished by Ann Tamaki Dion, Kix Edwin Kitow, Bob Yamashita, and Ken Yamashita. Martha and Eugene Uyeki also contributed their time by scanning materials and making their home available as a meeting site. Mary Jane Boltz and Jane Tomi Boltz helped to collect, collate, and create descriptions of the materials. Pat Boltz and Mary Marquardt have helped to gather War Relocation Authority files at the National Archives in Washington, D.C. Susan Yamashita Bowers transcribed Susumu and Kiyo Yamashita's diaries, and Hisaji Sakai transcribed many of the handwritten letters. Very significantly, Lucy Asako Boltz has worked most consistently with the growing archive, retrieving, digitizing, and organizing materials, and creating the archival website that holds this memory.

Through yearly grants from the Senate Committee on Research at the University of California, Santa Cruz, I have been able to travel to various national archival sites, and I am grateful for the support of librarians and archivists at many institutions: Wendy Chmielewski at Swarthmore College Fellowship of Reconciliation Peace Archives; Jaeyeon Chung at the Garrett Evangelical

Theological Seminary Library; Donald Davis and Barbara Montabana at the American Friends Service Committee Archives in Philadelphia; Christopher Densmore at Swarthmore College American Friends Library; Reverend James Hopkins at the Lakeshore Avenue Baptist Church in Oakland; Diane Peterson at the Haverford College McGill Library Quaker Archives Special Collections; Laura Russo at Boston University Howard Gotlieb Archival Research Center, housing the Howard Thurman Papers; and the Stanford University Hoover Institute. At my own institution at UCSC, I am especially grateful to bibliographer Frank Gravier and to Elizabeth Remak-Honnef, director of Special Collections at McHenry Library, where the Yamashita Family Archive will be finally housed and supported.

UCSC Senate COR faculty grants also made possible funding for research assistants who digitized and scanned materials for the website archive. I am grateful to Jonah Stuart-Brundage and Sebastian Honnef for their work, and especially thankful to Michael Jin, who created the initial website platform to house this archive. Thanks also to Alan Christy, Jay Olsen, Tosh Tanaka, and Angela Thalls for their guidance and technical support.

Very significantly, a United States Artist Ford Foundation Fellowship supported a year's sabbatical leave supplemented by funding from the Humanities Division at UCSC to complete the writing of this manuscript. I am very grateful for this generosity.

Today, the Yamashita Archive seems to me to be immense and varied, a large cache of hoarded stuff, now somewhat organized and curated. Several years ago, when my cousins discovered that my next project would be to tackle this growing archive, they arranged a reunion, ostensibly to visit Asako, but probably to check out what I would be writing. It's true; you should never trust a fiction writer. I had to admit that I wouldn't really be writing a family history, wouldn't be airing the laundry so to speak, that I had something more particular and narrow in mind. Maybe they were disappointed or relieved; in any case, someone else will have to write the great generational epic, not me. Ann Dion has written a family story of the Yamashita and Tamaki families as they arrived from Gifu, Tokyo, and Okinawa, and Ken Yamashita has meticulously researched the histories of Yamashita and Kitano families as well. If I need to check on particulars, they are my go-to family historians, and I'm indebted to their knowledge and support.

In the meantime, for this particular project, I've had special collaborations from very special friends. Early on, I met Alma Gloeckler and Olive Thurman Wong, whose memories are embedded in this work. And there are those scholar friends who unwittingly accepted dinner invitations, shared their stories and scholarship, or read early versions of these so-called *letters* as I stumbled around questions aroused, sometimes by only a short passage or fading photograph, in the immensity of this archive. I humbly thank: Bettina Aptheker, Anjali Arondekar, James Clifford, Gildas Hamel, Ruth Hsu, Lelia Casey Krache, James Kyung-Jin Lee, Boreth Ly, Roshni Rustomji-Kerns, and Mitsuye Yamada for your patience, your scrutiny and care. I apologize for my assumptions; the correspondent muses I've here created are my fictions to play with the gaps and speculations of this history and are entirely my fault.

As always, thanks to the excellent staff at Coffee House Press, in particular to Caroline Casey and Chris Fischbach, with special memories of Allan Kornblum. And grateful thanks to my literary support system at UCSC, faculty friends and staff, but especially to Micah Perks and Ronaldo V. Wilson.

In the interim between drafts and continuing edits of this project, cousin Ted Ono and cousin-in-law Eugene Uyeki have died. And so, too, my mother Asako, almost reaching this year the age of ninety-nine. For a short year, we enjoyed in our immediate home a household of four generations. I will miss this joyful commotion. My kids have said that the best times at home are when I'm writing, because *the house is clean and the food is great*. Which is to say that cleaning and cooking are how I get through the writing. But families with writers know the drill, that we writers spend a large space of time ignoring them or blabbing and waxing on about things of which they have no interest. And so, continuing thanks to my family—Jon and Angie, and Jane Tomi and Pat in L.A., who are always there to fill in for me on my trips away, and to the immediate Santa Cruz household: Ronaldo, Jane Tei, and Javon.

—Karen Tei Yamashita, August 2015

SELECTED BIBLIOGRAPHY

Adachi, Jeff (director), *You Don't Know Jack: The Jack Soo Story*, documentary film, 2006.

Austin, Allan W., *From Concentration Camp to Campus: Japanese American Students and World War II*, University of Illinois, 2007.

Benedict, Ruth, *The Chrysanthemum and the Sword: Patterns of Japanese Culture*, Meridian Books, 1967.

Clifford, James, *The Predicament of Culture: Twentieth-Century Ethnography, Literature, and Art*, Harvard University, 1988.

Cone, Margaret, and Richard F. Gombrich (translators), *The Perfect Generosity of Prince Vessantara: A Buddhist Epic*, Oxford, 1977.

D'Emilio, John, *Lost Prophet: The Life and Times of Bayard Rustin*, University of Chicago Press, 2003.

DuBois, W. E. B., *The Souls of Black Folk*, 1903.

Dutt, Romesh C. (translator), *The Ramayana and the Mahabharata*, Long J. M. Dent & Sons, EP Dutton & Co, New York, 1910.

Gandhi, Mohandas K., *Gandhi's Autobiography: The Story of My Experiments with Truth*, (translated from Gujarati by Mahadev Desai), Public Affairs Press, 1948.

Hamel, Gildas, *Poverty and Charity in Roman Palestine: First Three Centuries C.E.*, University of California Press, 1990.

Homer, *Iliad* (translated by Robert Fagles), Penguin Books, 1990.

Kitano, Harry, *Japanese Americans: The Evolution of a Subculture*, Prentice Hall, 1969.

Kroeber, Karl, and Clifton Kroeber (editors), *Ishi in Three Centuries*, University of Nebraska Press, Lincoln, 2003.

Kroeber, Theodora, *Ishi in Two Worlds: A Biography of the Last Wild Indian in North America*, University of California Press, 1961.

Okihiro, Gary Y., *Storied Lives: Japanese American Students and World War II*, University of Washington, 1999.

Radhakrishnan, S., *The Bhagavad Gita*, George Allen & Unwin, Ltd, 1948.

Said, Edward, *Culture and Imperialism*, Vintage, 1993.

Seow, C.L., *Ecclesiastes: A New Translation with Introduction and Commentary*, The Anchor Bible, Doubleday.

Smith, Lillian, *Strange Fruit*, Reyanl & Hitchcock Publishers, New York, 1944 (24th printing, Cornwall Press, New York).

———, *Killers of the Dream*, W. W. Norton & Company, 1949 (new edition, 1961).

Takemoto, Paul Howard, *Nisei Memories*, Scott & Laurie Oki Series in Asian American Studies, 2006.

Thomas, Dorothy Swaine, Charles Kikuchi, and James Sakoda, *The Salvage: Japanese-American Evacuation and Resettlement*, University of California Press, 1952.

Thomas, Dorothy Swaine, and Richard Nishimoto, *The Spoilage: Japanese-American Evacuation and Resettlement during World War II*, University of California Press, 1946.

Thurman, Howard, *Jesus and the Disinherited*, Beacon Press, 1976 (first published 1949).

———, *Deep River and the Negro Spiritual Speaks of Life and Death*, Friends United Press, Indiana, 1975.

———, *With Head and Heart: The Autobiography of Howard Thurman*, Harcourt Brace & Company, 1979.

LITERATURE
is not the same thing as
PUBLISHING

Coffee House Press began as a small letterpress operation in 1972 and has grown into an internationally renowned nonprofit publisher of literary fiction, essay, poetry, and other work that doesn't fit neatly into genre categories.

Coffee House is both a publisher and an arts organization. Through our *Books in Action* program and publications, we've become interdisciplinary collaborators and incubators for new work and audience experiences. Our vision for the future is one where a publisher is a catalyst and connector.

FUNDER ACKNOWLEDGMENTS

Coffee House Press is an internationally renowned independent book publisher and arts nonprofit based in Minneapolis, MN; through its literary publications and *Books in Action* program, Coffee House acts as a catalyst and connector—between authors and readers, ideas and resources, creativity and community, inspiration and action.

Coffee House Press books are made possible through the generous support of grants and donations from corporations, state and federal grant programs, family foundations, and the many individuals who believe in the transformational power of literature. This activity is made possible by the voters of Minnesota through a Minnesota State Arts Board Operating Support grant, thanks to the legislative appropriation from the arts and cultural heritage fund. Coffee House also receives major operating support from the Amazon Literary Partnership, the Jerome Foundation, The McKnight Foundation, Target Foundation, and the National Endowment for the Arts (NEA). To find out more about how NEA grants impact individuals and communities, visit www.arts.gov.

Coffee House Press receives additional support from the Elmer L. & Eleanor J. Andersen Foundation; the David & Mary Anderson Family Foundation; the Buuck Family Foundation; the Dorsey & Whitney Foundation; Dorsey & Whitney LLP; Fredrikson & Byron, P.A.; the Fringe Foundation; Kenneth Koch Literary Estate; the Knight Foundation; the Rehael Fund of the Minneapolis Foundation; the Matching Grant Program Fund of the Minneapolis Foundation; Mr. Pancks' Fund in memory of Graham Kimpton; the Schwab Charitable Fund; Schwegman, Lundberg & Woessner, P.A.; the US Bank Foundation; VSA Minnesota for the Metropolitan Regional Arts Council; and the Woessner Freeman Family Foundation in honor of Allan Kornblum.

THE PUBLISHER'S CIRCLE OF COFFEE HOUSE PRESS

Publisher's Circle members make significant contributions to Coffee House Press's annual giving campaign. Understanding that a strong financial base is necessary for the press to meet the challenges and opportunities that arise each year, this group plays a crucial part in the success of Coffee House's mission.

Recent Publisher's Circle members include many anonymous donors, Suzanne Allen, Patricia A. Beithon, Bill Berkson & Connie Lewallen, E. Thomas Binger & Rebecca Rand Fund of the Minneapolis Foundation, Robert & Gail Buuck, Claire Casey, Louise Copeland, Jane Dalrymple-Hollo, Ruth Stricker Dayton, Jennifer Kwon Dobbs & Stefan Liess, Mary Ebert & Paul Stembler, Sally French, Chris Fischbach & Katie Dublinski, Kaywin Feldman & Jim Lutz, Sally French, Jocelyn Hale & Glenn Miller, the Rehael Fund-Roger Hale/Nor Hall of the Minneapolis Foundation, Randy Hartten & Ron Lotz, Dylan Hicks & Nina Hale, Jeffrey Hom, Carl & Heidi Horsch, Amy L. Hubbard & Geoffrey J. Kehoe Fund, Kenneth Kahn & Susan Dicker, Stephen & Isabel Keating, Kenneth Koch Literary Estate, Allan & Cinda Kornblum, Leslie Larson Maheras, Lenfestey Family Foundation, Sarah Lutman & Rob Rudolph, the Carol & Aaron Mack Charitable Fund of the Minneapolis Foundation, George & Olga Mack, Joshua Mack & Ron Warren, Gillian McCain, Mary & Malcolm McDermid, Sjur Midness & Briar Andresen, Maureen Millea Smith & Daniel Smith, Peter Nelson & Jennifer Swenson, Marc Porter & James Hennessy, Enrique Olivarez, Jr. & Jennifer Komar, Alan Polsky, Robin Preble, Jeffrey Scherer, Jeffrey Sugerman & Sarah Schultz, Alexis Scott, Nan G. & Stephen C. Swid, Patricia Tilton, Stu Wilson & Melissa Barker, Warren D. Woessner & Iris C. Freeman, Margaret Wurtele, Joanne Von Blon, and Wayne P. Zink & Christopher Schout.

For more information about the Publisher's Circle and other ways to support Coffee House Press books, authors, and activities, please visit www.coffeehousepress.org/support or contact us at info@coffeehousepress.org.

Reissued Works by Karen Tei Yamashita

Brazil-Maru

Tropic of Orange

Through the Arc of the Rain Forest

KAREN TEI YAMASHITA is the author of *Through the Arc of the Rain Forest, Brazil-Maru, Tropic of Orange, Circle K Cycles, I Hotel,* and *Anime Wong,* all published by Coffee House Press. *I Hotel* was selected as a finalist for the National Book Award and awarded the California Book Award, the American Book Award, the Asian/Pacific American Award for Literature, and the Association for Asian American Studies Book Award.

Letters to Memory was typeset by
Bookmobile Design & Digital Publisher Services.
Text is set in Arno Pro.